D1617037

THE
WOLF
IN THE SOUTHWEST

THE
WOLF
IN THE SOUTHWEST
The Making of an Endangered Species

David E. Brown
Editor

Major Contributing Authors
Dan Miles Gish
Roy T. McBride
Gary Lee Nunley
James F. Scudday

THE UNIVERSITY OF ARIZONA PRESS
TUCSON, ARIZONA

About the Editor ...

DAVID E. BROWN in 1980 became a big game supervisor with the Arizona Game and Fish Department. Prior to that, he spent almost twenty years in a number of field positions with the agency. Brown has published numerous articles about wildlife in professional journals, including cooperative works on southwest vegetation and the effects of climate on wildlife populations. A member of The Wildlife Society and a fellow with the Arizona-Nevada Academy of Science, he has received several awards from conservation and professional organizations. Brown received a degree in wildlife conservation and management in 1961 from San Jose State College in California.

This publication results in part from the efforts of the U.S. Fish and Wildlife Service to document the history of the wolf in the Southwest. It incorporates the opinions and views of various people who contributed to or participated in the documentation process, but it does not necessarily reflect the opinions, philosophies, or policies of the U.S. Department of Interior, the U.S. Fish and Wildlife Service, the Mexican Wolf Recovery Team, or cooperating agencies or institutions.

Cover photograph taken by Francis Morgan at the Arizona-Sonora Desert Museum, Tucson, Arizona.

THE UNIVERSITY OF ARIZONA PRESS
The Arizona Board of Regents
All Rights Reserved

This book was set in 11/13 Quadritek Plantin
Manufactured in the U.S.A.

Library of Congress Cataloging in Publication Data

Main entry under title:

The Wolf in the Southwest.

Bibliography: p. 177
Includes index.
1. Wolves—Southwest, New. 2. Wolves—Mexico.
3. Endangered species—Southwest, New. 4. Endangered species—Mexico. 5. Mammals—Southwest, New.
6. Mammals—Mexico. I. Brown, David E. (David Earl),
1938– . II. Gish, Dan Miles.
QL737.C22W645 1983 599.74'442 82-17399

ISBN-0-8165-0782-1
ISBN-0-8165-0796-1 (pbk.)

Contents

   Physical Attributes   118
   Behavior and Habits   130
   Social Organization   139
   Reproduction   143
   Population Characteristics   148

4. Old One Toe and Other
   Famous Wolves   155

5. A Dire Prognosis   166

   Bibliography   177

   Index   187

ILLUSTRATIONS
Photographs

  Main Prey of Mexican Wolf   12
Wolf Runway Through Southern
  Arizona Woodland   23
Pine Forest in Sierra Madre Occidental
  in Mexico   28
Wolf Caught in Double Set Trap   33
Number 4½ Newhouse Trap   34
PARC Field Conference in Arizona in 1929 35
Successful Denning Operation   38
Early PARC Hunter's Kit   40
Biologist Vernon Bailey Around 1907   53
J. Stokley Ligon at Age 82   53

Figures

Maps

TABLES

A Word
From the Editor

LET ME SAY AT THE OUTSET that I have never seen a wolf in the wild—there are none left to see in the Southwest. Nonetheless, almost anyone who has camped and rambled there before the 1970s has a wolf story or two, and I am no exception.

I vividly remember one fine fall day in 1962. I was at the Arizona-Sonora Desert Museum near Tucson where a small group of us was shown a captive male wolf that had been trapped near Tumacacori, Arizona. At that time this was considered to be the only Mexican wolf in the United States. Plans were to breed him to a bitch that had been raised from a pup somewhere in Sonora, Mexico. Great expectations were anticipated for this forthcoming union: the Arizona-Sonora Desert Museum would be the world's source for Mexican wolf stock, and, who could say, eventually some descendants might be used to reestablish a wild population of lobos in the Southwest.

Several of us were gathered around the cage, which was stark and none too spacious, watching the wolf as it balefully watched us. It was a sorry-looking specimen—an emaciated animal with oversized head, ears, and feet and short hair that was matted and dingy. The animal was excited, and like so many captive creatures, he was pacing, almost running, from one side of his confinement to the other. The pungent smell of urine and feces remains in my mind, perhaps because there was a conspicuous recent deposit on the floor of the cage.

Some of us questioned whether this pathetic-looking beast was all wolf. Something in its pale yellow eyes told me it once may have been but was no longer. I watched the "wolf" for some time, feeling a mixture of revulsion and sadness. Years later, in March 1970, I saw a wolf hide nailed to the wooden side of a forestry office near El Salto on the Durango-Mazatlán Highway. Its large size and heavy brindled coat greatly impressed me. Could this be the same animal as the miserable creature I had seen in that cage? I couldn't say . . . there were no eyes to tell me.

A winter in the early 1960s also comes to mind. I could look up the exact date, but it doesn't matter. Ron Anderson and I were wildlife managers making bighorn sheep surveys in the Silverbell, West Silverbell, and Sawtooth mountains in southeast Arizona. One night, while camped near the northeast boundary of the Papago Indian Reservation, we heard the howling of a wolf. Although neither of us had ever heard a wolf before, we immediately knew what it was.

Local ranchers and ranchhands had heard it too and had found other evidence of its presence. Within a day or so, predator control agents had arrived with traps and "getters." Although no wolf was obtained, the howls and reports soon ceased. Some thought that maybe a "getter" had gotten him (it was always *him,* never her or it); or, since this was not wolf country, others believed he had moved on. No one ever knew his actual fate, but no wolf howls have been reported there since. Nor will they be. Soon the only wolf stories left to be told in the Southwest will be those that one conjures himself.

ACKNOWLEDGMENTS

This work is the result of the assistance and cooperation of many people. Jerry Burton and James E. Johnson of the U.S. Fish and Wildlife Service saw the value of such an effort and handled the administrative aspects that allowed and funded preparation of the manuscript and illustrations. To them and to Marilyn Hoff Stewart and Matt E. Alderson, who provided artwork, must go particular credit and thanks. Special credit goes to Curtis Carley, U.S. Fish and Wildlife Service, for contributing invaluable editorial review and willingly sharing his extensive knowledge of wolf biology and predator control practices. Many thanks also to Neil B. Carmony, Bob Housholder, Dirk V. Lanning, Dr. E. L. Cockrum, Dr. Lyle K. Sowls, and Dr. Inge Poglayen of the Arizona-Sonora Desert Museum, for their photographs, time, and expertise.

Dan M. Gish gave freely of his photos, his time, and

most importantly, his reservoir of experience and knowledge. These were crucial ingredients of this book over and above his written contribution. Thanks also to J. E. Hawley, of Phoenix, Arizona, for sharing his recollections of working with "wolfer" Albert Pickens and for contributing information on northern New Mexico.

Also helpful and assisting this effort were Terry Jackson and Thomas E. Waddell of the Arizona Game and Fish Department; Mrs. Helen Mercer; and Deene Mills and Duane Rubink of the U.S. Fish and Wildlife Service. Julie Miller, Joanne Littlefield, and Judy Claustre typed the manuscript, thus making this book a reality. Their work is highly valued.

Special credit is given to Norm Woolsey, John S. Phelps, W. L. Minckley, and especially Paul M. Webb of the Arizona Game and Fish Department for their editorial review. To them and to the other reviewers, Neil B. Carmony, Gale Monson and Marilyn Hoff Stewart, go my special thanks and appreciation.

My appreciation also goes to the University of Arizona Press for publishing this book. And last, I would like to thank Rose Houk at the University of Arizona Press. Her editorial expertise and organizational ability made preparation of the book an enjoyable exercise while producing a readable product.

DAVID E. BROWN

Background

THE WOLF IS ABOUT TO DISAPPEAR from the Sierra Madre as it has from so many other places—the Plains, the Rocky Mountains, the Great Basin in western North America, and numerous areas elsewhere. That the wolf was not completely eliminated much earlier from the North American Southwest is only due to a lack of concentrated effort to seek out the last remnants in the wilder parts of northwest Mexico. In few places in the world has the wolf been so much in conflict with a region's dominant land use as in the Southwest. Here the livestock industry has been united to have the wolf removed forever from its domain. Powerful political forces were mustered to enlist the aid of the U.S. government in the total removal of this premier livestock predator from western rangelands and to insure that no reservoir of breeding wolves remained for reinfestation. No refuge for wolves was to be permitted.

1

That this has essentially been accomplished does not mean that the livestock interests are to be chastised for their success. No group or organization opposed their singleminded purpose. Sportsmen and their associations, state game and fish departments, the U.S. Forest Service, and the U.S. Biological Survey all abetted the quest; almost none among them resisted it. Nor were naturalists and protectionists a factor in hindering the wolf's demise. No voice was raised for a rational and effective program to maintain a small but representative wolf population while one still existed. Anguish expressed in the late 1960s and 1970s over predacides and predator control came too late to benefit the wolf and would probably have had little effect in any event.

Thus, the Southwest's heritage of large national parks and monuments, wildlife refuges, and extensive wilderness areas was established and managed without the wolf. It is not possible to make the wolf howl part of a planned southwest wilderness experience. Whether a source of satisfaction or sadness, the wolf's extirpation from the Southwest is a fait accompli. That this passing did not go unchronicled is due to a remarkably few individuals. This book is their story of that extermination.

It is a great, if expected, irony that those who mourned the wolf's disappearance the most were the wolf hunters themselves—but then they knew the wolf best. Some kept detailed records of their observations and activities. One, Stanley P. Young, was so interested in wolves that as senior biologist for the U.S. Biological Survey he assembled all the known accounts of North American wolves and, with the eminent mammalogist E. A. Goldman, produced one of the first scientific treatments of this interesting canine. Their 1944 classic *The Wolves of North America*, long the definitive work on the subject, remains useful and readable today.

Young's early work with predatory animals was done in the Southwest, and much of the 1944 book pertains to this region. In fact, the predator control arm of the biological survey was instigated in the Southwest—primarily in New Mexico by Vernon E. Bailey, then staff biologist for the bureau's Biological Investigations Division, and J. Stokley Ligon, who became the first district inspector for the bureau's Predatory Animal and Rodent Control (PARC) Service in 1915. Bailey's (1931) discussions of wolves in his *Mammals of New Mexico* was one of the first by a biologist, and Ligon's early reports from 1916 to 1924, although laced with a strong hatred of wolves, contain the first factual statistics on wolves in the region.

Although some of the early PARC agents were wolf hunters, they were not biologists. Some were conscientious, ethical men, others were less so. In any case, those who continued any length of time had to show responsibility and be good at their profession: they had to know predatory animals and how to kill them. The best of them, especially in the early years before the PARC began to rely so heavily on predacides, were trappers, hound men, or both; almost all were good outdoorsmen, and a few kept careful notes of their observations.

Some of the more responsible agents later became inspectors and other district administrators. District supervisors filed periodic newsletters and annual reports summarizing the efforts of their hunters. These reports—summaries of C. F. Bliss (1921–1922), E. L.

Pineau (1923, 1926), E. F. Pope (1925–1926), A. E. Gray (1926–1929), W. C. Echols (1927–1928), J. C. Gatlin (1930–1938), C. E. Cates (1939–1941), and L. H. Laney (1942–1958) for New Mexico; and those of M. E. Musgrave (1919–1929), D. A. Gilchrist (1930), B. E. Foster (1931–1937), and E. M. Mercer (1937–1961) for Arizona are now particularly valuable.

G. L. Nunley (1977) succinctly summarized this and later New Mexico material for the U.S. Fish and Wildlife Service, and D. M. Gish (1978), under contract with the U.S. Fish and Wildlife Service, did the same with the Arizona reports. Both works are incorporated here, not only for their colorful narrative and descriptive photographs, but because Nunley recorded Arnold Bayne's firsthand accounts, and because Gish knew many of the principal people personally. This book is based importantly on their material and on Gish's observations, recollections, and collection of personal correspondence.

The Predatory Animal Control Service did not supervise its agents in Texas but instead cooperated with local governments and livestock associations and contracted with private trappers. Consequently, there is a paucity of data from the Trans-Pecos Texas portion of the Southwest. Those data available were presented by Scudday (1977), who provided the service with an excellent summary of the Mexican wolf in west Texas.

Control work on and near the Mexican border, particularly involving the use of Compound 1080, resulted in few if any wolves infiltrating across the United States-Mexico border after 1970. Wolf work could still be had in the Sierra Madres, however. Although this redoubt had been visited by some stellar biologists, including A. Starker Leopold (1959) who took notes (and a wolf or two) from a then unexploited population near the Río Gavilán, again it is a professional wolf hunter who best describes the remaining wolves in Mexico.

Roy T. McBride has a master's degree in biology from Sul Ross University and operates out of a ranch near Alpine, Texas. Fluent in Spanish and a rugged outdoorsman, McBride has traveled extensively in northern Mexico as a professional predator hunter. Although a hound man, McBride has obtained a considerable number of wolves as a trapper. When it became apparent that wolves were becoming increasingly scarce in Mexico, the Office of Endahgered Species of the U.S. Fish and Wildlife Service commissioned McBride to supply wolves for a captive breeding program and to document the known occurrence of remnant wolf packs in Mexico. Under contract, McBride (1978, 1980) then provided the U.S. Fish and Wildlife Service with an informative, professional report of his experiences with wolves in that country. Much of this book is based on his important findings, records, and photographs.

In the last two decades a number of scientific studies on wolf ecology and behavior have become available (for example, Burkholder 1959; Mech 1966, 1970, 1977; Pimlott 1967; Kolenosky 1972; Peterson 1977; and Skeel and Carbyn 1977). Equally informative but from a naturalist bent are works such as those by Mowat (1963). Although these have added to our understanding of wolves and their habits, all concern boreal wolves. A designed study of southwest wolf ecology or behavior has never been conducted and is now no longer possible. The U.S. Fish and Wildlife Service is to be commended for commissioning the works of Nunley (1977), Scudday (1977), Gish (1978), and McBride (1978). These reports and those of others who actually knew southwest wolves are becoming increasingly scarce. Like the wolves themselves, those who knew them will soon pass on, and this summation will remain as the main testimony of the wolf's presence in the Southwest.

SYSTEMATICS AND BIOTIC AFFINITIES

Early biologists placed great emphasis on subspecific and racial characters. This was especially true of mammologists, most of whom were also avid collectors. Each animal's physical characters were noted in detail and each geographic variant described as a new subspecies, or if possible, a full species. Even large, highly mobile forms such as wolves were thought by many to have numerous recognizable variants regardless of the reproductive continuity between populations.

In recent years there has been a tendency to combine or "lump" previously described taxa, and lower the systematic ranking of species to subspecies. Many of these systematic reorganizations were based on multivariate statistical analyses of skull measurements. A partial stimulus for these studies was the Endangered Species Act of 1973. This act gave great importance to previously described taxa—subspecies as well as species, the actual recognition of many of which were considered moot since the original descriptions were based on variable characteristics from small samples.

Although often showing the fallacy of previously described taxa, these systematic studies fail to recognize behavioral differences, habitat affiliations, or other potential isolating factors that differentiate groups of animals in their adaptations to regional environment. Such differences, if indeed real, are more than merely interesting, they are manifestations of evolutionary changes in the making—the recognition of which is the purpose of systematics.

Subspeciation, after all, represents evolutionary change in the making—plant and animal responses to isolating regional differences in habitats. Plant and animal community responses to integrated climatic factors within a particular geographic region are collectively recognized as biotic provinces (Dice 1943). These in turn are characterized by one or more biotic communities (biomes) that are natural plant formations composed of selected species presenting a distinctive vegetation physiognomy. Populations of plants and animals adapted to a particular biome or biotic province can be considered *biome-types*. Most subspecies, then, are biome-types.

Goldman (1944) recognized and assigned five subspecies or races of gray wolf in the Southwest: *Canis lupus baileyi* (Nelson and Goldman 1929), the Mexican wolf or lobo, found in Madrean montane forests, evergreen woodlands, and adjacent grasslands in Mexico, southeast Arizona, and extreme southwest New Mexico; *C. l. mogollonensis* (Goldman 1937), an "Arizona" wolf of Mogollon and sub-Mogollon Arizona and west-central New Mexico; *C. l. monstrabilis* (Goldman 1937), the Texas wolf of southwest

Texas, southeast New Mexico, and northeast Mexico; *C. l. nubilis* (Say 1823), the so-called Plains or buffalo wolf of the Plains grasslands, extending from Sas-katchewan, Canada, through the Oklahoma and Texas panhandles to northeast New Mexico and the Llano Estacado of New Mexico and Texas; and *C. l. youngi* (Goldman 1937), an intermountain or Great Basin form, inhabiting Utah, southern Wyoming, western Colorado, eastern Nevada,* down to northern Arizona and northern New Mexico (Map A).

Goldman's separation of these subspecies was based on size, pelage color, fifteen skull measurements and characters, and presumably biogeographic affinity. Goldman, who described four of the five subspecies, was a follower of the biotic province and community concept (see, for example, Goldman and Moore 1945), and the assignment of races to biomes would have seemed appropriate to him.

The native prey of the Mexican wolf was almost entirely the diminutive Coues white-tailed deer (*Odocoileus virginianus couesi*); the Arizona wolf would have fed on white-tailed deer and mule deer (*Odocoileus hemionus*), and on an occasional prong-horn (*Antilocapra americana*). The Texas wolf would have depended mostly on mule deer and pronghorn, with some Texas white-tails (*O.v. texanus*) and bison (*Bison bison*) in their diet. The natural prey base of the larger Plains wolf was reported to have been bison and pronghorn. *C.l. youngi* would have coevolved with the

---

*One specimen from the Providence Mountains in southeastern California may have been a straggler (Young and Goldman 1944).

Rocky Mountain mule deer (*O.h. hemionus*) as a principal food source. It appears likely that these different prey, along with the different habitats they occupied, could have indeed resulted in the subspeciation of wolves into biome-types as suggested by Pimlott (1967), Kolenosky and Standfield (1975), and Scudday (1977). Such evolutionarily selected differences, if real, would have broken down with the widespread introduction of livestock to the Southwest after 1880 and the reduction of native ungulates. Variations in behavior and habitat differences were never studied in the Southwest; most museum material postdates the universal introduction of livestock from 1880 to 1890 in Arizona and New Mexico and from 1910 to 1940 in northwest Mexico.

Bogan and Mehlhop (1980) conducted statistical analyses of 253 adult wolf skulls from the Southwest. Using twenty-five skull measurements, they concluded that of Goldman's five nominate subspecies, *baileyi* and *youngi* were the most recognizably distinct and that *mogollonensis* and *monstrabilis* represented intergrades between these two subspecies.

Bogan and Mehlhop's intergradation status of *mogollonensis* and *monstrabilis* is appropriate, but the inclusion of *mogollonensis* specimens north of the Mogollon Rim with *baileyi* appears forced. Female *mogollonensis* were closer to *youngi*, so that animals from below the Mogollon Rim are probably best included with *baileyi*. This would avoid the incongruity of wolves from the South Rim of the Grand Canyon being classified as Mexican wolves and would appear more compatible with biogeographic conditions.

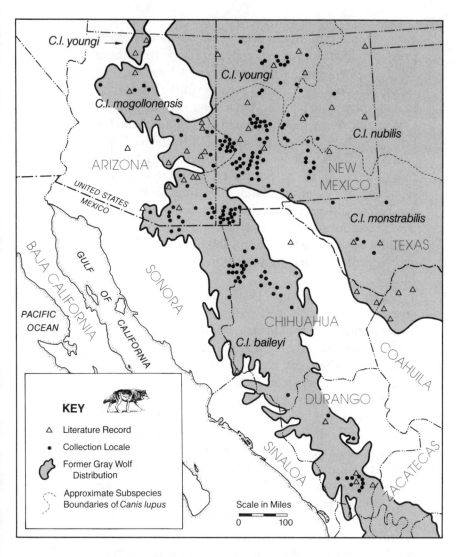

Map A. Historic Distribution and Records
of the Gray Wolf in the Southwest

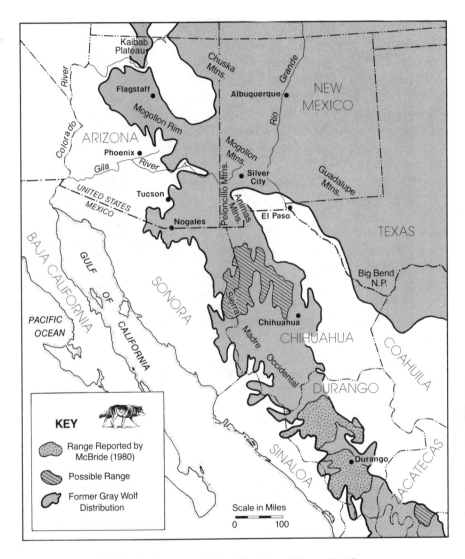

Map B. Presumed Distribution of Gray Wolf
in Southwest in 1980

11

Coues white-tailed deer in Madrean evergreen woodland, main prey and habitat of the Mexican wolf.

In summation, Goldman's nominate classification of five Southwestern wolves was probably sound. Although importantly based on physical characters, some of which like pelage show great variation, Goldman's races also show a general affinity with biogeographic considerations. That two of his five subspecies show intergrading characters with adjacent forms should come as no surprise and does not violate his taxonomic classification in toto. The importance of whether a particular specimen was a *baileyi*, a *mogollonensis*, or an intergrade, of course, is now largely academic.

1

The Long and Dismal Howl: Early Accounts

WOLVES HAVE BEEN PRESENT IN THE SOUTHWEST since at least the late Pleistocene. Their remains are well represented in the fossil record in Arizona (Lindsay and Tessman 1974) and New Mexico (Findley and others 1975), and wolf bones have also been identified from a number of the region's pre-Columbian archaeological sites (Martin and Plog 1973). The Big Game Hunters that appeared at the close of the Pleistocene some twelve thousand years ago (Martin 1963) must have vied with wolves for game. Men and wolves have been at odds ever since. It was not until the arrival of the Spaniards and their livestock, however, that conflict really began.

HISTORIC OCCURRENCE

By the end of the seventeenth century, cattle, sheep, and goats were being introduced to the Southwest in increasing numbers. Livestock, given to sedentary

13

Indians to raise, had to be continually protected from both Apaches and wolves. Describing conditions in northern Sonora in 1763, Jesuit priest Juan Nentvig (1763) wrote, "The wolves do damage among cattle, and the coyotes and foxes, among sheep and poultry."

Apaches and wolves quickly became addicted to this steady food source. Although a number of cattle ranches were established on large land grants, they were generally unprofitable because of these two forces. Apache raids sometimes resulted in the abandonment of many fine haciendas, with the cattle turned loose to the benefit of both predators.

The large, poorly guarded livestock herds of the Spanish and Mexican periods may actually have led to an increase in wolves. Certainly American explorers found wolves plentiful enough near what was to become the Arizona-Sonora border (Tyler 1964). In 1847 the Mormon Battalion found numerous wild bulls, remnants of some hundred thousand head of Andalusian cattle left behind when Rancho San Bernardino was abandoned in the 1830s; most of the more susceptible cows and calves had succumbed to predators, leaving only the large, formidable bulls (Tyler 1964 and Davis 1973). These and other cattle left behind on Mexican land grants generally disappeared by the 1860s (Wagoner 1952). Conditions were not entirely one-sided, however. Members of John R. Bartlett's 1849–1851 boundary survey noted that Mexican ranchers defended their stock against wolves and coyotes by lacing fresh livestock kills with strychnine (Baird 1859).

On entering the Southwest, American frontiersmen found wolves common if not particularly numerous.

Emory (1848) reported wolves on several occasions on the upper Gila River in New Mexico. In 1851 Bartlett (1854) described "wolves" as abundant on the plains and valleys of southern New Mexico, southeast Arizona, and northern Mexico. Although Bartlett, leader of the first U.S. Boundary Commission expedition, did not always differentiate between coyotes and wolves, he did list "the large wolf or lobo" as one of the large mammals of the mountains and riparian groves of the rivers and creeks of the Southwest.

Early American boundary and railroad route surveys were usually accompanied by naturalists, who kept accounts of wolves both from the thinly settled Mexican areas and in the wilderness. These accounts, though brief, provide valuable insights into the abundance and distribution of wolves when the Southwest was in a natural or nearly natural state.

The first naturalist to travel extensively in the Southwest was S. W. Woodhouse, a physician with the Sitgreaves expedition of 1851. Captain Lorenzo Sitgreaves and his party traveled west from Santa Fe, down the Zuni and Little Colorado rivers, across north-central Arizona and southern California to the Pacific coast. Dr. Woodhouse, in his biological report of the expedition, found wolves "very common throughout the Indian territory [Oklahoma], Texas, and New Mexico" [Arizona was then still part of New Mexico Territory] (Sitgreaves 1853).* Woodhouse found wolves particularly common on the thin, open grasslands west of San Francisco Mountain in Arizona.

---

*These may have included coyotes. Wolves and coyotes were not always differentiated in early accounts. The tendency to call coyotes "wolves" in Texas and the Plains states can also be confusing.

A more descriptive account was given in 1853 by C. B. R. Kennerly, naturalist and physician with a railroad route survey along the thirty-fifth parallel. Traveling much the same country that Woodhouse had traversed two years earlier, Kennerly discussed the natural history of the region of the Zuni and Little Colorado rivers in east-central Arizona:

> At night the prairie jackal or coyote rarely failed to approach our camp, and serenade us with his loud and varied notes. The long and dismal howl of the larger species [wolf] was occasionally heard in the distance; but the latter is much less numerous than the former, and was not often seen. It, too, prefers the wooded regions, and depends mainly upon the deer for subsistance, which it hunts, and rarely fails, after a long pursuit, in overtaking and conquering (Kennerly 1856).

This account is of more than casual interest considering later opinions on the exclusivity of coyotes and wolves, since it has the two species existing together under pristine conditions.

During the winter of 1853 and 1854, Kennerly and H. B. Möllhausen (1858) noted that the men of the Whipple party, while camped on the Little Colorado River near Chevelon Creek, entertained themselves by trapping wolves and hunting. One night their remuda of mules was stampeded by a pack of wolves howling close to camp. Later on the same trip, west of Mt. Sitgreaves, Möllhausen (1858) noted:

> Here and there we saw solitary specimens of the black-tailed deer and antelope, and more frequently wolves and coyotes announced their presence by howling and

chattering as they prowled around us in the scanty cedar woods. A wolf was also seen on Partridge Creek and others heard in the foothills of the Juniper Mountains.

Kennerly was again involved in southwestern exploration in 1854 and 1855, as the naturalist accompanying the Emory expedition surveying the new United States-Mexico boundary created by the Gadsden Purchase. Kennerly made notes concerning wolves:

> Near Santa Cruz, in Sonora we found this animal more common than we had observed it elsewhere on our route. It, as well as the coyote, were often destructive to the flocks around the village (Baird 1859:15).

Kennerly also observed a large number of coyotes west of the Rio Grande, howling nearly every night near camp. Thus, his notes indicate that coyotes apparently coexisted with wolves in early rural Sonora.

The first naturalist to reside for a significant period in the Southwest in presettlement times was Elliot Coues. A surgeon in the Army, he was stationed at Fort Whipple in central Arizona, near present-day Prescott, in 1864 and 1865. While in Arizona, Coues traveled a good deal, collecting specimens and gathering natural history information from soldiers, hunters and trappers. His *Quadrupeds of Arizona*, published in 1867, is the first attempt at a comprehensive treatment of the mammals of the region. Concerning wolves Coues wrote:

> They are common enough about Fort Whipple, though shy and wary, and seldom making their appearance by day; and notwithstanding their size and imposing

appearance, the part they played was insignificant
compared with that of their smaller relatives, the coyotes.
. . . This latter animal . . . is by far the most abundant
carnivorous animal in Arizona, as it is also, in almost
every part of the West (Coues 1867).

On one occasion Dr. Coues noted a mixed chorus of
coyote and wolf howls:

> A short sharp bark is sounded, followed by several
> more, in quick succession, the time growing faster and
> the pitch higher, till they run together into a long
> drawn lugubrious howl in the highest, possible key. The
> same strain is taken up again and again by different
> members of the pack, while from a greater distance the
> deep melancholy baying of the more wary Lobo breaks
> in, to add to the discord, till the very leaves of the trees
> seem quivering to the inharmonious sounds (Wheeler
> 1875).

Coues (1867) also reported that a number of wolves
taken in winter were grizzled white and that many had
been poisoned for their fur, which made fine robes.

That the wolf was never especially numerous in the
Southwest is suggested by the paucity of place names.
There is no Wolf Mountain or Wolf River, no Sierra
Lobo or Rio Lobo. Wolf Creek Pass in Colorado and
the two Wolf creeks in the Bradshaw Mountains near
Prescott, Arizona come to mind. The largest of these
creeks is perhaps so named because one Daniel Ellis
Conner (1956) saw a large pack of wolves there in
1863.

With the return of the Army to the Southwest after
the Civil War, the Apache menace was gradually

reduced and then eliminated. Transcontinental railways begin to penetrate the country, providing a link to eastern and California markets. By the late 1880s, the region was relatively settled, and cattle were abundant and widespread. Wolves were conspicuous if not abundant, and their conflict with ranchers was acute. W. W. Price, a zoological collector in southeast Arizona, observed in 1894 that the lobo "is the terror of the cattle and sheep men. . . . It is found over the entire region, though more especially in the mountainous parts. We saw it on several occasions during our stay in the country" (Allen 1895). To rid the Southwest of this "terror," a campaign requiring more than sixty years and millions of dollars was mounted—an effort almost as great as that devoted to neutralizing the Apaches.

FORMER DISTRIBUTION

Except for the so-called buffalo wolves or loafers (*Canis lupus nubilis*) reported to inhabit the grasslands of Texas and eastern New Mexico, wolves in the Southwest generally have been associated with montane forests and woodlands (Bailey 1931, McBride 1980). Almost all collections have come from pine-clad mountains, oak woodlands, pinyon-juniper forests, and intervening or adjacent grasslands above 4,500 feet (Map A). Surprisingly, virtually no wolves have been recorded in California despite an abundance of what appear to be suitable habitats (McCullough 1971). Wolves were also largely absent from the Mohave, Sonoran, and Chihuahuan deserts; wolf records from Arizona and Mexico are almost entirely above the elevations of desertscrub and even semidesert grassland.

Evidence that wolves did not frequent the originally open semidesert grasslands is provided by Scudday (1977) who quotes Judge O. W. Williams of Fort Stockton, Texas. Williams was educated at Harvard, came to Texas as a surveyor in 1877, and noted all that he observed. In 1884 he opened a law office in Fort Stockton and later became judge of Pecos County. In 1908 the *Fort Stockton Pioneer* published a series of Judge Williams's observations on the county's animal life. An excerpt from that series offers interesting insight into the early status and distribution of wolves in that part of the Trans-Pecos:

> . . . these animals are not now and have never been numerous in our country. Twenty-five years ago there was said to be one pack of lobos in Pecos County. They ranged on the Pecos River about 30 miles above Sheffield. Then, as now, they depended upon herds of cattle for sustenance. The cattle of "S" and Mule Shoe brands were the principal prey of this pack. Cattle had been introduced into Pecos County only a short time before, and I am unable to say whether or not the lobo made its appearance here before we brought cattle. Early settlers believed that it came here after the cattle appeared. I am disposed to think, for several reasons, that this was probably the case.
>
> As its English name "timber wolf" indicates, the wolf prefers to inhabit wooded country and forests. Our area is a land of plains. We have no forests, trees are exceedingly rare, and coverts of small brush are infrequent. The country was even more sparse 25 years ago. There must have been good and sufficient cause to bring the wolf into the type of environment that animals avoid. It wouldn't be too puzzling if an abundance of food were present. Within historic time the buffalo doesn't appear to have ever been abundant in this section. The deer and antelope were not copious, and were also animals capable of escaping wolf's pursuit.

Apparently in early times, nature did not allow for the wolf in the economy of this country. But when cattle moved in, large herds ranged over an immense area of the unfenced country. With such huge herds and vast pastures, cattlemen could give their herds only minimal protection. The cattle were necessarily turned loose to fend for themselves.

This condition was favorable to the appearance and increase of the lobo population. Though the forest and glade were absent, the mesas and the rocky caverns around the mesa furnished shelter for the lobo. . . .

Such conditions allowed the lobo to extend its range. First we began to hear of its ravages at the Tunas Spring, 22 miles east of Fort Stockton. Then we heard of it about the old Neighbors ranch, 40 miles south of Fort Stockton. Later, it became troublesome in the foothills of the Glass Mountains both on the north side and the south side. Very early, the wolf marked himself a well-defined area of territory in which it is always found. Ravages outside this territory are rare and transitory.

The northern and western end of the country have remained free from lobos. These portions are fairly level, destitute of caves and good hiding places, and are without mesas or rocky hills. But the southern and southeastern parts of the county are land with high, but small table lands separated by valleys of various widths. Here, the lobo has found a congenial home and safe retreat. If a straight line were drawn on the Pecos County map from Househead Crossing on the Pecos River to the Glass Mountains, this line would mark approximately the northern and northwestern limits of damage done by wolves.

Because of their natural hunting method of running deer to ground, southwestern wolves probably avoided rough, precipitous, and brushy terrain. Most reports indicate that they frequented high mountain ridges, rounded hills, mesas, bajadas, and wooded stringers extending into grassland valleys. These accessible landscapes contributed to the wolf's demise since they allowed wolf hunters and their pack animals to cover wide areas.

Since wolves regularly traveled between mountain ranges, occasional stragglers occurred outside this regular range. With the ubiquitous prey base offered by livestock introductions, individual wolves may have operated far from their normal haunts. Old Aguila was such a wolf, ranging the Sonoran Desert and semidesert grasslands north and west of Wickenburg for eight years before being poisoned in 1924. Wolves were also reported on the Papago Indian Reservation in southwest Arizona (Young and Goldman 1944, Gish 1978). Roy McBride (1978) reported taking what he considered a transient pair of wolves in the Chihuahuan Desert north of La Ascensión, Chihuahua. Such individuals were unusual, however, and the wolf's range in the Southwest has generally been overstated.

Arizona

In southern Arizona the wolf regularly ranged as far west as the Madrean evergreen woodland in the Baboquivari Mountains. George Ballesteros, who worked on the Redondo Ranch, stated that the last resident wolves in the Baboquivaris were trapped in 1943. He recalled that at least one of these was a female and, like other wolves he remembered, she did not cower like a coyote but met the trapper's club vicious and defiant to the end.

The Santa Rita, Tumacacori, Atascosa-Pajarito, and Patagonia mountains were all well known as wolf country, as were the Canelo Hills. At least equal numbers inhabited the steeper and rougher, but larger

This wolf runway in Madrean evergreen woodland in the Pajarito Mountains, and others like it in southern Arizona's Ruby Country, were where many of the last wolves were taken in the state.

Chiricahua, Huachuca, and Pinaleño mountains. A number of wolves were also recorded from the Catalina Mountains—some of them as recently as the 1950s (Lange 1960). All these mountain ranges were, and are, good Coues white-tailed deer country.

Northward, wolves ranged through the oak- and juniper-studded mesas and broken chaparral-covered hills of Greenlee, Graham, Gila, and Yavapai counties through the Apache Indian reservations and the Mogollon Rim. Here the Mexican wolf integrated with the so-called Arizona wolf of the Mogollon highlands.

These wolves extended west from the New Mexico boundary through the forested Escudilla and White mountains, along the Mogollon Rim and Coconino Plateau, to the San Francisco Peaks, Kendrick Mountain, and Bill Williams Mountain. From here small numbers of wolves reached northward to the South Rim of the Grand Canyon and westward to the pinyon-juniper woodlands as far south as Peach Springs (Young and Goldman 1944).

Still further north and to the east one might have encountered wolves, presumably the intermountain variety *youngi*, on the ponderosa-covered Defiance Plateau and in the Lukachukai and Chuska mountains of the Navajo Reservation. This race of wolves extended north into the Manti-LaSal and Blue mountains of Utah and beyond. A few wolves also occupied the North Kaibab Plateau until the mid-1920s before being brought to justice by the U.S. Biological Survey (Rasmussen 1941, Russo 1964). Since they fed primarily on the then dense population of Rocky Mountain mule deer, it is ironic that the wolves were removed from this national game refuge at a time when the excessive number of deer was a great concern to national forest administrators. According to the late D. I. Rasmussen, the last wolf in this part of northern Arizona was taken on the Paria Plateau about 1928.

New Mexico

Wolves were widespread in New Mexico. Findley and others (1975) cite museum specimens and literature records for almost all counties west of the Pecos River. Even the Staked Plains had some wolves, and

New Mexico is the only state to have what Goldman (1944) considered all five races of southwestern wolves. Knowledge of the distribution of wolves in this state comes mainly from the annual PARC reports of J. Stokley Ligon (1916 to 1924), his successors, and Vernon Bailey (1931).

As in Arizona, wolves west of the New Mexico plains were most prevalent in high mountain country capped with conifer forest. The literature shows wolves as especially common, or at least persistent, in the Mogollon Mountains and the adjacent Elk, Tularosa, Diablo and Pinos Altos mountains, in the Black Range, and in the Datil, Gallinas, San Mateo, Mount Taylor, Animas, and Sacramento mountains. Almost all the mountains higher than 6,000 feet with ponderosa pine forest had some wolves. Elsewhere wolves occasionally ranged through open glades next to cedar breaks, wooded ridges, and tablelands. These habitats were occupied northward in a broad front into Colorado. Only in the low desert areas of the state were wolves transient or absent.

Wolves had been essentially eliminated in New Mexico by the mid-1920s. Only in Hidalgo County's Animas, Peloncillo, and San Luis mountains did wolves persist into the 1930s—their constantly depleted ranks continually refurbished by new recruits crossing the Mexican border along long-established runways (Young and Goldman 1944). This is where government hunter Arnold Bayne continued to take wolves each year until the 1950s when the use of Compound 1080 eventually eliminated the trans-border stock. The last wolf "taken" in New Mexico was a carcass reported by Bayne (1977) from the Peloncillo Mountains in October 1970.

Trans-Pecos Texas

Although wolves once roamed a large area of the Trans-Pecos, the only museum records are from the Guadalupe Mountains (1901), twenty miles southwest of Marfa in Presidio County (1942), Davis Mountains (1944), Cathedral Mountains (1970), and south of Longfellow near the junction of Terrell, Pecos and Brewster counties (1970) (Scudday 1977). Interestingly, the first two specimens were classified as the subspecies *monstrabilis*, the three later animals as *baileyi*. This led Scudday to suggest that the Mexican wolf was not native to the region and had wandered in from Mexico. It may also be instructive to note that the *baileyi* specimens were found the farthest southeast and were the ones most closely associated with Madrean evergreen woodland.

Literature references place wolves in the Davis and Glass mountains but not in the Chisos Mountains in Big Bend National Park. Wolves almost certainly occurred there, however, since some were taken near Terlingua (Stevens 1979). Wauer (1973) cites that the La Harmonia Company at Castolon, a long defunct town on the Rio Grande, processed and shipped east fifty wolf hides in 1925. Although these could have originated in the interior of Mexico, it seems reasonable to expect that at least some were obtained locally.

Coahuila—Sierra Madre Oriental

The former distribution of wolves in the outlying ranges of the Sierra Madre Oriental is uncertain. The only museum specimen from northeastern Mexico is one obtained by Lt. D. N. Couch, probably from naturalist Luis Berlandier's collection housed in Matamoros, Tamaulipas. This location, in the tropics, is almost certainly not the origin of this animal (Bogan and Mehlhop 1980, McBride 1980).

Although Marsh (1937) reported wolves as common in the Sierra del Carmen vicinity, Taylor and others (1945), Baker (1956), and Leopold (1959) reported wolves scarce there. Other references to wolves in western Coahuila are provided by Baker (1956) and Leopold (1959) for the Sierra de las Cruces, Sierra de los Hecheros, Sierra del Pino, and Serranias de Burro. Both Baker (1956) and McBride (1980) refer to wolves on the desert plains southwest of Musquiz in the shadow of the Sierra Musquiz. McBride (1980) knew of wolves formerly occurring in the Sierra Rica, Chihuahua. These mountain ranges are all clothed in chaparral, Madrean evergreen woodland, and some pine forest. As elsewhere, the wolf was largely associated with temperate uplands and wooded habitats.

There are no records of wolves from eastern Coahuila, the Cerro San Luis Potosí in Nuevo León, eastern Zacatecas, or the Sierra Madre Oriental proper, but Dalquest (1953) reported wolves in the Mexican state of San Luis Potosí and examined one there. From the state of Veracruz there are several pre-World War I references, and one specimen from Mount Orizaba. This last record is the only one from the Transvolcanic District and is the southernmost museum record. Never numerous in eastern and central Mexico, wolves are now almost certainly extinct everywhere in Mexico except in the Sierra Madre Occidental.

Wolf habitat in the Sierra Madre Occidental, Chihuahua, Mexico. The forest along the crest at about 6,900 feet is almost entirely ponderosa pine.

Sierra Madre Occidental—Chihuahua, Durango, Sonora, Zacatecas

The Sierra Madre and its high outlying ranges and valleys, such as the Sierra del Nido, Sierra de las Tunas, Valle Santa Clara, and Valle Chuichuipa, have long been known as wolf strongholds. It was here, near Galeana, Chihuahua, that the specimen used to describe the Mexican wolf subspecies was collected. This long, blue ridge on northern Mexico's horizon represented the largest continuous area of wolf distribution in the Southwest. It was also from the northern limits of the Sierra Madre Occidental, in the San Luis and Guadalupe mountains, that wolves continued to invade Arizona and New Mexico long after resident wolves had been extirpated in the southwestern United States.

The wolf's wide range once included, and in small part remains, most of Chihuahua and Durango west of the Chihuahuan Desert and semidesert grasslands, extreme northwest Zacatecas, and the eastern edge of Sonora from 3,500 to 5,000 feet. In northeast Sonora, wolves are known to have occurred in the Sierra Pinitos; the Sierra Cibuta and surrounding hills, ridges, and peaks; and in the Sierra de los Ajos. Again, most records are in or near montane pine forests or evergreen woodlands (Brown and Lowe 1980). Wolves avoided steep barrancas and tropical-subtropical locales, preferring the high interior valleys, undulating ridges, and gentle slopes.

If the lobo has any useful qualities or habits, I have not yet learned of them. If it destroys any noxious animal, reptile or insect in appreciable quantity, I have no account of it. It seems to be a specialist in carnage and to have brought professional skill to the slaughter of cattle. Possibly it has its uses—but it will require a skillful man with a very high powered magnifying glass to ascertain them.

O. W. Williams, 1908

2

And None Shall Remain: Destruction of the Wolf

THE ARRIVAL OF ANGLO CATTLE RANCHES in the South-west in the late 1870s and 1880s meant an end to the frontier and the beginning of incessant warfare on the wolf. With the Southern Pacific, Santa Fe, and other railroads providing access to markets, the ranges were taken up and by 1890 cattle raising had become a competitive business. The numerous livestock provided a ready food source and, like the Indians, wolves had become dependent on livestock for sustenance. The wolf may have even temporarily increased its range, if not its numbers. Livestock predation became a serious matter.

Before this time, wolves had been killed largely for their pelts, as trophies, or as nuisances. Many of these were taken for the fur trade by using strychnine, although this practice was more prevalent in the Plains than in the Southwest (Young 1944).* This changed as the conflict with ranchers intensified. Wolves were killed by any means feasible, not for fur or sport, but simply to "clean them out."

EARLY CONTROL METHODS

Skilled hunters could sometimes track wolves in snow or locate a den, thus obtaining a shot at a wolf. Hunters often found it more productive to situate themselves near a livestock carcass and shoot wolves that came in to feed on the dead animal. Because of the wolf's endurance and the often level terrain, dogs could seldom be used to advantage as they could in hunting lions. One of the more widely and successfully employed techniques against wolves was poisoning; strychnine was commonly used, and in a few instances arsenic was selected, especially by Basque sheepherders and Mexican vaqueros. "Denning" was also effective, but the most important method was trapping with steel leghold traps—primarily the No. 14 Newhouse.

Traps

The most reliable and effective tool used by professional wolf hunters was trapping, although traps were often used in combination with poison. Wolf traps came in a number of types and sizes, and the type used depended on individual preference and agency policy.

---

*Wolves were never especially valued for their fur in the Southwest. The price of their pelts followed the erratic vogues of the fur market. When prices were good, as they were in the 1920s, bootlegging for pelts or bounties by PARC agents was not uncommon. Ligon (1919) mentioned "trappers being responsible for furs caught."

Wolf caught in a double set trap in Sycamore Canyon, Santa Cruz County, Arizona. The wolf probably stepped into the second trap while fighting the first. Note the trap's toothed jaws.

The most popular trap and the one used by many early U.S. Forest Service rangers and biological survey predatory animal agents was the double spring, No. 4½ Newhouse. This trap, developed in the 1890s, was available at hardware stores throughout the West (Young 1944). Basically an enlargement of the No. 4 beaver trap, it weighed 5¼ pounds and had an 8¾-inch jaw spread. Later, the No. 4½ Newhouse was supplemented by the No. 14 Newhouse and the No. 114 Newhouse with a larger, offset, toothed jaw.

A Number 4½ Newhouse trap. This was the main tool of "wolfers" from about 1912 through the 1930s and even into the 1940s and 1950s.

Other varieties of steel traps (some hand-forged) included double-jaws, double and single "leaf" springs, and coil-spring traps. Also called jump traps, coil-spring traps were credited with making a number of legendary "one-toed and three-legged" wolves.

A lengthy description of wolf trapping methods was given by Young (1944), but all southwestern trappers practiced their own variations. After the government got into predator control, numerous conferences were held in remote areas, where trapping techniques were to be discussed and shared.

One amusing aspect of these meetings was the district supervisor's effort to get his more successful trappers to demonstrate personal trap-setting methods. Rarely did one of the veterans volunteer. More likely, when the

time came, he would have a pack mule with a sore
back, gear that needed mending, or a trail hound with a
split foot.

Although the innate cunning of resident pack wolves
was greater than that of migrants far from home territories, the wolves' sharp instincts demanded the best
trap-setting skills and techniques. The trick was to stay
ahead of the rapidly moving wolves and second-guess
their next theatre of operations with trail sets.

Donald Gilchrist, Bureau of Biological Survey

PARC field conference in Apache County, Arizona,
in 1929. From left, PARC hunters Bill Ramsel and
Bud Davis; Mark E. Musgrave, Arizona district
superintendent for PARC; Arthur Young; a Mr.
Brown; Paul G. Redington, chief of PARC, Washington, D.C.; R. Lee Bayless, state game warden;
and Stanley P. Young.

Veteran hunters like Bill Casto insisted that they never bothered to bait a wolf trap. Their main concern was where the trap was set. Said Casto: "I want to get a wolf to step automatically into the trap *before* he has time to think about the bait."

Scent posts were an important factor in wolf trapping, however, and social scents were used in some form by most trappers. Albert P. Rhodes (1940) had a basic recipe, with variations of it used by several wolf hunters:

> Take eight coyote glands (or wolf)
> ¼ liver with gall
> 1 kidney
> black coyote or wolf dung (black from eating meat diet)

> Grind glands, liver with gall, and kidney, place in glass jar, screw lid on but do *not* seal air tight. Let stand in a warm place until well rotted. Then dissolve black dung in warm water and add two ounces of the well-rotted glands. Then it is ready for use. Scent trap every five days. Substitute wolf dung for coyote and wolf urine for the warm water if available. Mr. Williams (Harry P. Williams–Custer Wolf) says that coyote or wolf urine mixed with the dung is better than warm water. Also, in preparing the bait, be sure never to let flies blow the mixture. This always spoils it.

> (S) Albert P. Rhodes

Another wolf hunter of high repute and success gave his formula for wolf scent bait but requested anonymity:

> Take all parts of the wolf or coyote that is not flesh: internals [entrails], kurnals [sic]; glands; tongue; windpipe; lungs; eyeballs; brains; spinal column and

pads of feet and one-fourth pint of wolf or coyote gall.
Put this mixture in a five-gallon container, adding three
gallons of warm water. Cork tight and let set three
days in a warm place. Wrap an old blanket or quilt
around container at night if weather is cool, to prevent
chilling. Loosen cork each morning to release gas
pressure. It is ready to use the fourth day. Now, use a
gallon jug for mixing one-half pint of the base mixture,
25 drops of spirits of asafetida (use eye dropper), 2
drops of anise oil, 2 drops of tonquin musk (grain), 20
drops of Canton musk. Put this mixture in a gallon jug
and fill the jug with dog, coyote or wolf urine. When
using, do not use more than 20 drops at any one time
and not oftener than three times a week.

I have caught as many as three coyotes in one set
before rebaiting. This bait has laid under three feet of
snow for 90 days, and when the snow and ground
thawed, catches [wolves] were made just the same as
before the snow fell.
    If this [formula] is published, please do not mention
any names or state.

A trapper would make a set where he found a scent
post—scratch marks in the soil next to a bush, stump, or
clump of grass where wolves urinated to announce
territorial boundaries.
    Other equipment and tools used to trap wolves
included shovels, trowels, tweezers and surgical for-
ceps, Number 9 steel wire, diagonal wire cutters, bolt
cutters, setting clamps, and the inevitably necessary
"numbing club."

Denning

    "Denning" means simply locating active dens and
destroying the pups. Wolfers knew that most pups were
born in late April and that den sites, once used, were

An unidentified hunter performs a successful denning operation. This litter was much larger than average.

reluctantly abandoned. With trail dogs and knowledge of where to look, experienced hunters found denning an effective control technique. Once located, digging out the pups was hard work, requiring removal of much earth and rock (Young 1944: 319). By 1925, however, the "art" of denning dwindled with resident wolves virtually gone in the Southwest.

Strychnine

Traditionally, early southwestern fur trappers carried poison in their kits, and arsenic was a standard item among the trade goods at Santa Fe. Treating skinned-out beaver carcasses with poison to reduce wolves and lessen depredations on trapped beaver was common practice. Strychnine, a derivative of the nux vomica bean, later came into wide use as a canicide and a standby in predatory animal control. Wolf hunters used strychnine in various forms, and its effect on wolves was termed catastrophic (Musgrave; Gilchrist; Foster; and others).

In the heyday of wolf slaughter, from 1890 to 1925, several methods of strychnine poisoning were employed. Most common was "lacing" carcasses of prey animals that wolves were suspected of killing. Substantial wolf sign was normally evident at such sites, and kills were readily identifiable. Wolves most frequently pulled their victim down from behind, usually in the flank or rump areas (McBride 1977), while lions kill by breaking the neck or smothering the prey. Dispensing strychnine in molded suet cubes was standard practice for PARC hunters. Private and government hunters also habitually treated recognizable wolf-killed carcasses with "raw" strychnine in sulphate form—the specially processed one-grain alkaloid tablets or gel-coated tablets (Musgrave 1921, Gilchrist 1930). These encapsulating techniques sought to mask the strychnine in a wrapper of fat so that a canine, gulping the bait whole, could not detect the bitter quinine taste of the poison (Ligon 1924).

Early PARC hunter's kit: trap on left; dies (on either side of poison can) for molding suet cubes, and lidded can for carrying strychnine-treated cubes. Pack was used to carry equipment when hunter was on foot.

Strychnine was particularly effective in cold weather. Catalogued and mapped "drop baits" were distributed spokelike from an unpoisoned section of animal carcass that was wired down to a solid base to prevent the "station" from being dragged and scattered. To protect from raven theft, drop baits were usually concealed under a cow chip, a flat rock, or a piece of wood. When canines smelled the bait, their natural reaction was to snatch the morsel and quickly devour it.

Strychnine undoubtedly was responsible for a large percentage of wolves taken. Its actual role in reducing wolf numbers will never be known since many, perhaps most, animals taken by this method died unnoticed far from bait stations. Despite encouragement from government administrators, some agents, particularly the older ones, were hesitant to rely on strychnine or other toxicants. Many were hound men who appreciated the danger to dogs. They were also reluctant to use a technique that might prohibit them from obtaining a pelt, which might be bountied or serve as a trophy to their prowess.

From an economic standpoint lethal chemical control eased administrative funding problems, especially when man-hour costs rose during periods of economic depression or when transportation shortages plagued the PARC. Steel traps required the attention of a man setting and "running" each individual trap. One trap could catch only one predator at a time and had to be reset or retrieved. Chemical canicides, on the other hand, could kill dozens of animals with less man-hour expenditure than setting a trap line. The advent of civilization in the Southwest and the nonselectivity of strychnine, however, were its eventual undoing. Also, wolves and other predators learned to avoid strychnine. But the wolf's foes did not give up easily. Strychnine was replaced by more lethal and selective toxicants.

BEGINNING OF THE FEDERAL CONTROL PROGRAM—1890 TO 1915

By the late 1880s the Southwest was one large livestock ranch. Sheep were now on the range and cattle were so numerous that overgrazing was rampant. The year 1890 was deficient in rainfall and the following two years were almost devoid of the summer rains that were needed to nurture perennial grama grasses. In 1893 the livestock industry collapsed. Overgrazing and drought resulted in the loss of from 50 to 75 percent of the cattle in Arizona, according to the governor's report to the secretary of interior in 1896. Due only to rains that fell in the summer of 1893 was the industry saved from total ruin (Bahre 1977), but continued overgrazing and vagaries in the market made cattle raising a marginal enterprise, a condition that lasted through the 1930s. To make matters worse, the large numbers of dead and dying cattle offered conditions that favored wolves, and many considered this species to be more abundant and widespread in the 1890s than at any other time (Young 1944, Scudday 1977).

With ranchers going "belly-up" in profusion, every livestock loss could be shattering. Rustlers and wolves were hated because their depredations could mean the difference between survival and failure. A 1908 passage from O. W. Williams, the literate judge of Pecos County, casts light on the situation in Texas:

> Of all predators which prey upon our herds and flocks in 1908, the lobo inflicts the most damage, and causes stockmen the most trouble. It is not that it causes any sudden, large loss, but it is a constant, steady source of loss. It is not a calamity, such as the hordes of locusts and grasshoppers which have devastated the West a few times. It is more like a grievous tax that is laid on year by year, which must be borne with patience, and is counted every year as an entry in the volumes of profit and loss (Scudday 1977).

Until this time the rancher and his hired help were the principal means of predator control. When they were out on the range, all ranch hands carried a Winchester

30-30 or similar repeating rifle; any lion, bear or wolf encountered was shot at. Ranch boys ran trap lines for sport and extra money. Shepherds close-herded their sheep with guard dogs. Quick to learn, the wolves soon became wary.

When things got particularly out of hand, and if the owner could afford it, the ranch foreman would assign a man or hire a professional hunter to "thin out the varmints." Strychnine, arsenic, and traps were the usual tools of the trade. Only the largest spreads could afford a full-time varmint hunter, and the age-old bounty system, which paid the hunter according to his catch, became increasingly popular. The bounty system, always a favorite with the livestock industry, was especially attractive if payment could be dispersed by the local livestock growers association, or even better, by county or state governments. Political conditions were such that government disbursement was often used in the southwest United States and northern Mexico. Although the effectiveness of bounties has often been criticized, they indisputably led to reductions in large predator populations. Most wolves in the Southwest were killed during the 1890 to 1915 period when the use of bounties was widespread (Bailey 1931, Young 1944, Scudday 1977).

In 1893 the Arizona–New Mexico Territorial legislature passed the Territorial Bounty Act, which allowed counties to appropriate money for the payment of bounties on "predatory wolves, big bears [grizzlies], mountain lions, bobcats and coyotes." Thus, this first official measure against wolves was patterned after similar actions adopted by almost every state in the United States and Mexico (Young 1944).

Although authorized and "on the books," actual appropriations were something else. Bounties were costly and difficult to administer. Counties were characteristically short of cash, so livestock growers consistently lobbied for state bounties.* Some state legislators considered bounties a form of rural welfare and the responsibility of the livestock growers. Nevertheless, by 1914 the western states were paying out more than a million dollars a year in bounties (Young 1944).

Both public and private bounties varied depending on the abundance of the animal and economic conditions. Bounties by ranchers often included bed and board for the hunter; payment for wolves could range from $10 to more than $50 for particular animals (Gish 1978). Also, if the pelts were prime, and if only the

---

*It took all the political pressure the Arizona Cattle Growers, Arizona Wool Growers Association, and Arizona Livestock Sanitary Board could muster in 1932 to persuade Governor Sydney P. Moeur to provide predator control money from luxury tax revenues. (The state contribution to the federal government had been discontinued.) Even then, none of the money could be used for bounties; the $10,000 allocation was to employ one full-time lion hunter and two men to work solely on coyotes for the U.S. Biological Survey. Not until June 1947 did the eighteenth Arizona legislature reappropriate $15,000 a year to be spent as cooperative funds for predator control work. At the same time, the legislature passed a revision of the 1893 Bounty Law and appropriated $10,000 a year from general funds by which the livestock sanitary board *could* pay a bounty of $3.50 on coyotes, and $50 on wolves and mountain lions (later increased to $75). Effective July 1, 1947, the board elected to pay a bounty only on mountain lions. The next year the board included wolves, and eight privately taken wolves were bountied in 1948 and 1949. Only three "wolves" were bountied by private trappers in the next ten years. The last wolf bountied by the Arizona Livestock Sanitary Board was taken in August 1960 on the Schilling Ranch north of Willcox.

scalp needed to be turned in to collect the bounty, additional money could sometimes be made on the fur market. Gish (1978) reported what an economic boon wolfing could be for those who chose it as a profession.

In 1909, William S. Casto was employed to hunt wolves in southwestern Colorado, agreeing to work for a bounty of $50 per wolf, paid by the Club Ranch. So costly were the depredations of a particular wolf and so grateful was the Club Ranch management, that on the Spring Creek wolf's demise Casto was presented with a new .35 caliber Winchester lever-action rifle.

According to Casto, the bankruptcy of his cattle ranch on the Blue River in Arizona was due to wolf depredations in 1911 on his herds on their way to market. It was this loss that set the young Mormon cattleman on a life of wolfing and private contract hunting of other major predators.

In October 1913 another hunter-cowboy, Giles Goswick, was involved in the annual roundup of cattle in the high western Mogollons. When the crews found dead cattle "laying everywhere," Goswick was relieved of his roundup chores and employed by the local cattlemen to kill wolves for a bounty of $50 an animal.

Goswick went home, gathered his trail hounds, provisions, horses and traps, and returned to the kill site. Riding along a limestone ridge, he came in sight of a pair of adult wolves and their pups in dense timber. When the bitch wolf barked at his trail hounds, he shot her and four of the five pups. Remaining in the vicinity another five days. Goswick killed thirteen more wolves—a total of eighteen which earned him $900 for a week's work.

In 1914 J. Stokley Ligon, son of a Texas sheep
rancher, was employed by the biological survey to map
prairie dog colonies on the pioneer Becker ranchlands
near Springerville, Arizona. Ligon found several
wolves feasting on Becker livestock, so he caught two
wolves in traps he had set. August Becker paid Ligon
a $10 bounty for each wolf. Thus Ligon embarked on
a career in predator control—a career that was to be
bad medicine for the wolf.

That wolf and other bounties were paid in Texas
counties is documented by Scudday (1977), who found
the following reference in minutes of the Pecos County
Commissioner's Court, dated 14 May 1895:

> On this day the following named persons presented to
> the court scalps of wild animals, and the clerk was
> instructed to issue necessary warrants in payment-of-
> bounty as same as follows:

George Bennett	6 lobos	11 panthers	11 cayotis	$48.00
Juan Torres		2 panthers		5.00
Macedonio Luga			4 cayotis	2.00
Eulalio Fuentes		1 panther	8 cayotis	6.50
Jno. Stapleton			28 cayotis	14.00
J. B. Armstrong	1 lobo		11 cayotis	8.00
Frank Teel			6 cayotis	3.00

By 1905 wolves had been much reduced in the open
country of Texas and eastern New Mexico; only remnants remained in the Pecos Valley and none were left
in the Taos Valley and in the Jemez Mountains. Bailey
also reported wolves as troublesome, although less
common than formerly, in the Manzano, Capitan, and
Bear Springs mountains in New Mexico. They were
then still considered common in the Datil and Gallinas

mountains and abundant in the Gila National Forest (Mogollon, Black, Elk mountains) and in the Chuska-Lukachukai mountains (Bailey 1931). Wolves were less a problem in Arizona but still a force to be reckoned with.

A number of western ranchers and their congressmen requested that the U.S. government do something to alleviate the stockmen's plight—at least to the extent of studying the effects of wolf damage on the industry. They argued that it was particularly unfair for the administrators of the newly created national forests to collect grazing fees without providing any protection from wolves, which were mostly found in the forest reserves. This argument probably prompted Vernon Bailey, staff biologist for the U.S. Biological Survey, to write a bulletin in 1907 for the Department of Agriculture titled *Wolves in Relation to Stock, Game and the National Forest Reserves*. This publication was accompanied by another, *Directions for the Destruction of Wolves and Coyotes*, in which Bailey reported on conditions and provided a prescription:

> The enormous losses suffered by stockmen of the western cattle ranges and the destruction of game on forest reserves, game preserves, and in national parks through the depredations of wolves have led to special investigations by the Biological Survey in cooperation with the Forest Service, to ascertain the best methods for destroying these pests. The results appear in the present report, which includes also field notes on the distribution, abundance, and breeding habits of wolves.
>
> The chief object of the report is to put in the hands of every hunter, trapper, forest ranger, and ranchman directions for trapping, poisoning, and hunting wolves

and finding the dens of young. If these directions are
followed it is believed that the wolves can be so
reduced in number that their depredations will cease to
be a serious menace to stock raising. Prime wolf skins
are worth from $4 to $6 each, enough to induce
trappers and enterprising ranch boys to make an effort
to secure them if a reasonable degree of success is
assured. Stock owners need little encouragement to
catch or kill wolves on their own ranges, and it is
believed that the forest rangers will be able to keep
them down on the forest reserves. Their complete
extermination of the western range is not, however, to
be expected in the near future, and it is only by
constant and concerted effort that their numbers can be
kept down sufficiently to prevent serious depredations.

Needing to build a constituency that would favor reten-
tion of the forest reserves in federal ownership, the
Forest Service eagerly joined the predator control effort.
The first government predator control agents were forest
rangers and guards. The next year Bailey (1908) reported the results of the Forest Service effort in Arizona
and New Mexico: 232 wolves taken in New Mexico
national forests, 127 in national forests in Arizona.
Wolf catches would never be as high in these two
southwestern states again.

Bailey's bulletins were significant because they
correctly pointed out the need for a long campaign if the
wolf was to be brought under control. This line of
reasoning was also necessary to set the stage for a
government-sponsored control program that need not
be cost efficient. The last few wolves must be eliminated
regardless of the cost because it was the holdouts that
caused wolves to be a recurring problem. Bailey (1931),
describing conditions around 1905, indicates why the
bounty system did not eliminate wolves:

For a few years the loss of stock was much reduced, and the wolves through the region were too scattered to make professional trapping for the bounty profitable, although large bounties were paid by both counties and local stockmen. The lapse in vigorous trapping after a few years brought back the wolves to their original numbers. . . .

Wolves had to be eliminated from their more inaccessible hideouts. When wolf numbers were reduced to the point that bounty hunters could no longer make a go of it, the hunters moved on or took up other pursuits. High reproductive capability, coupled with the high numbers of easily obtained prey, allowed wolves to make a quick comeback.

That this was true is indicated by Henry Boice, long-time co-manager of the huge Chiricahua Cattle Company in the Black River region of the San Carlos Apache Indian Reservation:

. . . One great source of loss to us was the stock killed by wolves every year. In order to cut down this loss, we encouraged hunters to go into our range and catch them, paying $25.00 a piece bounty and furnishing them provisions. For a number of years, these bounty hunters caught from 15 to 25 wolves a year, but apparently, the number of wolves running on our range remained about the same (Gish 1978).

The bounty system had other drawbacks. An affidavit of a bounty paid in Pecos County, Texas in 1913 to R. C. Marchbanks illustrates some of the problems encountered (Fig. 2.1). Two kinds of wolves were recognized in addition to coyotes, and one wonders what some of these animals actually were. On his affidavit, Marchbanks claimed one lobo wolf, two gray

Pecos _____ County, Texas

To ___ R.C. Marchbanks, _____ Dr.

For Scalps of Wolves and other Wild Animals, as follows:

No. Killed	DATE KILLED Mo. Day Year	WHERE KILLED	ANIMALS		AMOUNT
1	Jan 2 1913	Holmes Ranch, Pecos Co.	Lobo Wolves	@$5.00each	5.00
			" "	@$5.00each	
			" "	@$5.00each	
2	Feb 26 1913	Holmes Ranch, Pecos Co.	Grey or Timber	@$5.00each	10.00
			Wolves	@$5.00each	
			" "	@$5.00each	
1	Jan 2 1913	"	Panthers	@$5.00each	5.00
			"	@$5.00each	
			"	@$5.00each	
			Mexican Lions	@$5.00each	
			" "	@$5.00each	
			" "	@$5.00each	
			Tigers	@$5.00each	
			"	@$5.00each	
			"	@$5.00each	
			Leopards	@$5.00each	
			"	@$5.00each	
			"	@$5.00each	
4	Feb 7 1913	Holmes Ranch, Pecos Co.	Coyote Wolves	@$1.00each	4.00
			" "	@$1.00each	
			" "	@$1.00each	
			" "	@$1.00each	
			" "	@$1.00each	
5	Feb 12 1913	"	Wild Cats	@$1.00each	5.00
			" "	@$1.00each	
			" "	@$1.00each	
				TOTAL	$29.00

THE STATE OF TEXAS
County of _____ Pecos _____

BEFORE ME H.L. Winfield, a Notary Public

_____ in and for _____ Pecos _____
County, Texas, on this day personally appeared R.G. Marchbanks,
_____ known to me, who being duly sworn, states on
oath that the foregoing and annexed accounts is true and correct, that it is unpaid,
and that he and no other killed the animals above enumerated
(Signed) R.G. Marchbanks

Sworn to and subscribed before me this 27th day of March A.D. 1913.

(Signed) H.L. Winfield
Notary Public, Pecos County, Texas

Approved by the Commissioner's Court the _13_ day of _May_ 191_3_
ATTEST:
(Signed)Frank R. Voney   (Signed)Neswell Johnson
          County Clerk   County Judge

Figure 2.1. Copy of bounty ledger and affidavit
used in Pecos County, Texas in 1913

or timber wolves, a panther, four coyote wolves and five wildcats. As the ledger indicates, the judge disallowed the gray wolves and credited them as coyotes.

Scudday (1977) includes other affidavits from Pecos County claiming wolves in 1912 and 1913; by 1915 the effort to eradicate predators must have begun to heavily tax the county's bounty fund. The following year the Pecos County Commissioner's Court instituted stricter controls:

> April 10, 1916—On this day it was ordered by the court that the clerk be instructed to issue warrants on the Scalp Bounty Fund of the County, to all persons having claims filed and passed on March, 1916, terms, in half the amount filed for, or in other words for only the County's one-half the claim; except however, the claims of W. R. Penninger, A. F. Johnson, J. A. Moore, W. W. Brewton, J. L. Broom and R. L. Pyeatt, whose said claims are held up in order that claimants may make showing to this court that all animals on whose scalp they base their claims, were actually caught in Pecos County, Texas.

Although the bounty system proved popular and could temporarily reduce predator numbers locally, it was prone to a number of abuses. Not the least of these was the hunters' tendency to shop around for the best price, regardless of the source of the catch. Apparently the identification of scalps was a problem and fraud was common. In 1909 Bailey published a key to help bounty payers differentiate wolves, coyotes, dogs, and other animals submitted for payment.

Arizona and New Mexico had attained statehood in 1912, but there was as yet no game and fish commission or department in either state. Sportsmen were becoming active and organizing, however, and in 1914 a game

protective association was organized in New Mexico.*
Sportsmen now joined the livestock interests in advocating a federal control program as the only real solution to the predator problem. Forest guards were
controlling wolves and other predators, but apparently
not with the required enthusiasm.

J. Stokley Ligon, a protege of Vernon Bailey, was
then working in the Southwest for the U.S. Biological
Survey. An ardent "conservationist," he actively took
up the cause against predators and was joined by others,
including a young forest ranger named Aldo Leopold.
In 1914 and 1915 they stumped the Southwest promot-
ing game laws, game refuges, and predator control.
Leopold, who was to change his mind about wolves
more than once,† then believed (as Ligon always did)
that predator control was an essential route to game
abundance.

These efforts were successful, and on June 30, 1914
the U.S. Congress made the biological survey responsible for experiments and demonstrations in destroying wolves, prairie dogs, and other animals injurious to
agriculture and animal husbandry. The sum of $125,000
was appropriated for 1914 and 1915, and 300 hunters
were immediately employed. Ligon and Leopold
harangued the sportsmen to throw all their support
behind the survey and *insist* that the job be completely
finished—to the last wolf and lion, lest these "vermin"
regain their range. (The words were Leopold's, the fear

---

*An Arizona game protective association was not organized until 1923.

†In later years, as head of the Wisconsin Game Commission, Leopold
voted to reinstate a bounty and control program against the handful of
wolves remaining in that state, despite his public acknowledgment that
they posed no threat to the state's burgeoning deer herd that he was then
attempting to reduce (Flader 1974).

Vernon Bailey in photograph taken around 1907. A respected senior biologist with the U.S. Bureau of Biological Survey, Bailey is best known for his contributions to the survey's North American Fauna series. He also founded the federal predator control program by successfully bringing the U.S. Forest Service into wolf control.

J. Stokley Ligon, at age 82, shortly before his death in 1961. Ligon, or as he was popularly called, Stoke, dominated New Mexico wildlife conservation for four decades. Most often associated with predator control and restocking, Ligon was also among the first to recognize and publish the devastating effects of overgrazing on wildlife.

Bailey's and Ligon's.) By the close of fiscal 1916, the western rangelands had been organized into control districts under competent supervisors with adequate field personnel. The inspector for the New Mexico–Arizona district was J. Stokley Ligon.

West Texas, having no public lands and a tradition against federal involvement, apparently did not form a control district, but instead continued to rely largely on local control efforts. Meanwhile, revolution had broken out in Mexico, and the ranching industry there was in a chaotic state. Wolf control, never actively pursued in Mexico, virtually ceased, providing temporary refuge for wolves in the Southwest.

EXTERMINATION—THE "FINAL SOLUTION"—
1915 TO 1925

Ligon wasted no time getting the Predatory Animal and Rodent Control (PARC) branch of the Bureau organized and functioning. An expert hunter and trapper, he used his $20,000 budget to hire hunters with a reputation, including about a dozen "wolfers." Some of the best were E. E. "Eddy" Anderson of Douglas, Arizona, who was to work the southeast corner of Arizona and Hidalgo County in New Mexico; Jack Hays; and Eddie Ligon (no relation to Stoke). Hays was to catch 71 wolves in 768 working days, but he worked an area where "wolves was everywhere"—the V T Range in the Mogollon Mountains and the Black Range in west central New Mexico.

The first year Eddy Anderson and T. T. Loveless took 4 adult and 7 young wolves in the Animas Mountain area, and a den of wolves was taken in the nearby Peloncillo Mountains by another government hunter, Bert Smith. Eddie Ligon claimed the first wolves in Arizona in the Cherry–Mingus Mountain area and in the rugged Fossil Creek region. During that first short year of operation, the PARC took 33 adult wolves and 36 immatures (pups and fetuses) in New Mexico and Arizona for a claimed total of 69 for the district (Fig. 2.2).

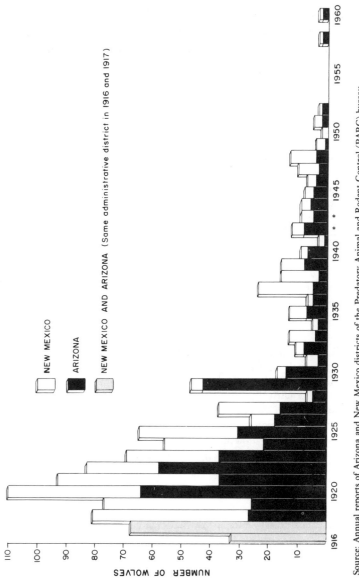

Figure 2.2. Wolves reported taken by federal and state cooperative hunters in Arizona and New Mexico, fiscal years 1916 through 1960

Source: Annual reports of Arizona and New Mexico districts of the Predatory Animal and Rodent Control (PARC) bureau
Note: May include some questionable wolves and wolves not discussed in PARC narratives
*Estimates

Ligon (1916) outlined a battle plan for the following year, with the ravages of the wolf his main concern. Because he estimated that 60 percent of wolf damage in the district occurred in New Mexico, he concentrated on that state:

> I think it a very conservative estimate when I place the number of adult gray wolves, in New Mexico, at the close of Fiscal Year at 300. If each of these wolves average the killing of three (3) cattle, anywhere from calves to grown stock, or their equivalent in horses or sheep per month, which is also a moderate estimate, means that each of these wolves gets 36 head of stock a year, or a total of 10,800 head per year. Valuing these stock at $30.00 per head, we find that it cost that high sum of $324,000.00 annually to feed this wolf pack alone.

Sixty-eight adult wolves and 17 pups were taken by PARC personnel in the district in fiscal 1916–1917 (Fig. 2.2). Ligon (1917) considered these good results:

> While we have not carried on the wolf work so extensively in Arizona as we have in the state of New Mexico, we have done some good service in Arizona and it is with pleasure that I state that it is my belief, that at least fifty per cent reduction in damage done by wolves has been accomplished in New Mexico, during the last twelve months. My estimate is that there are not more than 70 adult gray wolves in the State of New Mexico, at the present time, and perhaps that same number in Arizona.*

---

*Ligon estimated 300 wolves in New Mexico at the close of the previous year; with only 68 adult wolves taken by PARC hunters, either cooperators and other hunters took a considerable number of wolves, or Ligon's estimate was incorrect.

> At the time the government operations were begun,
> the V-T was the worst infested cattle range in the
> Southwest, and while there are still a few wolves in this
> range, they have been reduced so in numbers by our
> hunters that they cease to be very much of a menace
> any more. Since October 1915, we have caught in the
> V-T range alone, 28 wolves and 12 young.

After the onset of World War I, demand for beef was high and prices were good. In 1917, when the United States entered the war, demand for range beef increased further. Ligon, Leopold, and other wildlife enthusiasts used the war to justify an intensified predator control effort. Any cattle losses meant dollars and cents from the war effort, they argued.

At a conference in Albuquerque on November 1, 1917 an estimate of "damage" to the livestock industry caused by "wolves, mountain lions, 'big' bears [grizzlies], coyotes, bobcats and wild dogs" during the preceding year in New Mexico was compiled:

	Number of Head	Value
Cattle	24,350	$1,374,000
Sheep	165,000	1,320,000
Horses	850	21,250
		$2,715,250

These figures were repeated in speeches throughout the Southwest, and the practice of estimating livestock damages by predatory animals in large dollar figures quickly became common. The PARC administrators really believed in their mission: more was better; predatory animal control work cost money—for supervision, clerical and field personnel salaries, and equipment and material. It was the death knell for wolves because these figures would be used to justify the program's economics on an "estimated" basis, rather than on more objective cost-benefit analysis.

Control efforts intensified in 1918; 81 adult wolves and 30 pups were taken in the district, PARC's largest take to date (Fig. 2.2). Between February 6 and June 30, 1918, another 12 wolves were poisoned by a special force employed by New Mexico A & M College (Gish 1978).

Nothing short of extermination was the game plan. Ligon made this clear in an optimistic summary of conditions in mid-summer 1918:

> My experience, while operating in the field, has developed two outstanding facts; the gray wolf will be exterminated throughout the west within reasonable time; and the control of coyotes—a far larger task—is dependent on the application of swifter methods than trapping.
>
> The big wolves have been so reduced in numbers in New Mexico and Arizona that they no longer confront us as a serious menace. We hope to have the remaining forty or fifty animals in New Mexico run down before the winter weather interferes with the work. It is very probable that wolf work can be continued up to Christmas. By that date there will be less than a dozen in the State. The best hunters are being kept constantly after these animals. At the present time, there are but one to three of the animals remaining together, and their wide range and shyness make their capture prolonged and uncertain.
>
> There was probably in the neighborhood of $100,000.00 worth of damage done by lobo wolves in the District during the past fiscal year. More than half of this amount was confined to New Mexico—or about $60,000.00. . . . The damage during the past year is rather evenly distributed over the State, perhaps the

greatest losses occurring in the Carson, Jemez, and
Gila National Forests—although quite a lot of cattle
have been killed in the Mescalero Indian Reservation,
in the Sacramento Mountains and in the Jicarilla Reservation, northwestern New Mexico. Two or three wolves
still remain in each of these reservations. . . . Very few
wolves lived to get away from the dens the past spring
in New Mexico. This signifies that there will never be
any more young raised to maturity in the State unless it
be along the Mexican border, and this line will be carefully guarded in the future for animals that may drift in
from Mexico (Ligon 1918).

Ligon put great faith in a chosen few to carry out his
goal of complete elimination of wolves. Only a few were
considered painstaking and enthusiastic enough to meet
his standards:

Credit for the wolves that have been killed and those
yet to be killed must go to a dozen men. We have been
fortunate in holding our good wolf hunters. Two are
now in the Army Service, Mr. W. A. Mullins, and
Mr. Eddie Ligon. The more our operations expand and
the more men we experiment with, the more I am
convinced that successful wolf hunters are rare.
There is no use in trying to develop a man for such
work who is not cautious and painstaking, or who is
lacking enthusiasm. We have really discovered material
for but three wolf hunters during the last twelve months,
although a dozen men have been tried out. This being a
fact, I feel that much reliance must be placed in a few
chosen men to carry out this important line of work to
a successful conclusion in good time.

Despite the skill and success of his hunters, Ligon had
overstated his previous, optimistic predictions. In 1919,
somewhat disappointed, he reported:

Dispensing with the gray wolf in the State has been
prolonged beyond time anticipated by the Inspector.
Inability to keep the best hunters constantly after the
animals, weather conditions, and the permitting of pups
to escape from dens, are factors that have aided the
animals in their fight. Invasion from other states, and
especially from Mexico, also had considerable bearings.

It is a practical impossibility to prevent increase so
long as there is a pair of wolves at large, although they
may be old, minus toes or entire feet, or carry wounds
made by bullets. Such afflictions have no serious bear-
ing on prolific reproduction—with the single exception
of age.

There are probably a dozen adult wolves in the State
at the end of the fiscal year, not including those that
enter and leave over the border; but this number is
probably increased one hundred per cent by pups that
have not been taken this season. This means that thirty
wolves will have to be taken during the first half of the
coming year in order to make the finish.

. . . The damage now being committed in the State is
so small, compared to previous years, that little complaint is heard. However, adults that remain are costing
$2,000.00 each, or at the rate of $24,000.00 annually.

Seventy-eight adult and 19 pup wolves were taken in
the two-state area that year—only a few less than the
previous year when Ligon reported the wolf all but
eliminated. Clearly the war was yet to be won.

During fiscal 1918–1919, New Mexico and Arizona
were split into separate districts. Mark E. Musgrave was
appointed inspector in Arizona and Ligon remained
New Mexico inspector. Costs had burgeoned, and the
PARC budget for both states for the fiscal year was
approximately $57,000, almost triple its original budget
of 1915–1916. This amount included $12,576 from the

federal government for Arizona, matched equally by the state, and $31,677 for New Mexico. Such an increase in expenditures would be examined carefully during the postwar recession. Ranchers were queried to state their losses in writing. Four hundred forty-five stockmen and farmers reported $378,151 in livestock losses in Arizona alone. Others reported a loss of 2 to 10 percent of their calf, colt, and lamb crops. Using the 2 percent figure, Musgrave (1919) calculated the annual loss in Arizona from predatory animals at more than $1.5 million.

Using what he called "widely accepted" estimates, Ligon (1919) figured that a potential livestock loss of $265,000 in New Mexico was averted—for a mere expenditure of $31,000. With such favorable statistics, it is no wonder that most ranchers heartily supported the control program (Fig. 2.3).

The wolf campaign was to be carried on vigorously in both states. Musgrave was determined to make a special effort to kill wolves, hybrids, and a pack of wild dogs ranging along the Arizona-Mexico border. He initiated a concentrated program against wolves reported to be ranging on the watersheds of the Black River, Eagle Creek and Blue River, and in the White Mountains on Bonita Creek. Regarding the status of wolves in Arizona, Musgrave (1919) noted, "Wolves are not numerous in this State, but are scattered over a very large area, and there are a great many individuals [wolves] that cover a big range and are very shy."

In his *Summary Report of Operations with the New Mexico State Council of Defense, February 6, 1918 to December 31, 1919,* Ligon stated that "depredations by wolves have been reduced by three fourths" since

Walnut Wells, N. M.
Alamo Huecco Ranch,
May 23, 1919

Mr. J. S. Ligon
Predatory Animal Inspector
Albuquerque, New Mexico

Dear Sir:

  I have been thinking ever since T. T. Loveless was ordered away from here that I would write you and ask you to send us another trapper, but have been somewhat backward about it, inasmuch as the territory in which you have this trapping done is a large one, and so few men to trap. I figured we would be asking too much to ask again for a trapper, and now I am glad we didn't for since Loveless left here we caught two lions and one lobo wolf—the lions after they had each killed a colt, and the lobo in a trap on a trail. All these were good catches, and it seems to have got them, as we see no more sign, but no doubt there will be others soon to come in to the range.

  I wanted to tell you that T. T. Loveless you had here was pure and simple a trapper, and deserves all the credit of such. He sure knew what a wolf was thinking about when he saw his tracks the day following and could come near telling just when he would be back to the traps, and kept them set. If we ever catch a lobo we will have our money back for the traps, even if we don't get the trap back. If we only snapped the trap on a lobo, and say he got off with the trap, we would be ahead. We would be rid of the wolf, for he would finally die with the trap hung to him, and I believe this plan will greatly help to thin out the lobos and lions also.

  Ever thanking you for the work done in here by you,
I remain.

Very truly yours,
(Signed) R. V. Moorehead
Manager "V" Ranch

Figure 2.3 Copy of letter supporting wolf control program

November 1, 1917. He repeated his belief that the
wolves in Arizona and New Mexico were no longer a
serious menace, but added that "trapping the remaining
wolves is going to be a long, drawn out process."
  Of 78 wolves taken during fiscal 1918–1919, 15
came from the Arizona-Sonora border and 8 were
taken from the White Mountain country. Musgrave
stated that "when operations stopped in May, there were
few or no wolves left on this side of the border." Ligon
estimated that probably a dozen wolves remained in
one-tenth of New Mexico. Two hundred sixty adult
wolves had been taken in the two states by the PARC
since operations had begun on September 15, 1915.
  The next year, 1919–1920, 110 adult wolves and at
least 21 young wolves were reported taken by the
PARC in New Mexico and Arizona—a new record
(Fig. 2.2). Clearly, predator numbers were as difficult
to arrive at then as they are now. An apologetic but ever-
hopeful Ligon (1920) recognized that much work
remained before the war would be won:

> The wolf situation is one that will require intensive or-
> ganized effort until the last animal is taken, not only
> in Texas and New Mexico, but in every state where
> they find suitable harbors and when this is accomplished,
> we will have to guard the gateways to Mexico so long
> as there is a supply in that country. The gray wolf tribe
> will die hard to the last hybrid, and long after we think
> we have them out of the way, they will make their
> appearance. It is first nature with the wolf to ramble,
> and to cover distance with speed is one of his enjoyable
> pasttimes. The mountainous regions of the west are not
> entirely in keeping with his nature and for this reason
> he is not particularly attached to any one district—food
> and protection being the two things sought. Wolves have
> not yet been entirely eliminated in any region of the

west where there is suitable protection in which they have established themselves. Where both sexes of their species have not been able to survive, hybrid off-spring is the result.

Progress against the remaining gray wolves of the State was up to expectations during the past year, taking into consideration curtailed operations caused by limited funds.

While it is now rather early to make predictions regarding the increase, it is not probable that any young will reach the age of maturity. July 1st, there was known to be no more than 12 wolves that make their home wholly in the State. In addition to these, one family or more of hybrids is in the Black range. The survivors are easily giving way under our trapping methods.

Damage due to predatory animals the past year to domestic stock alone, in New Mexico, was less by one-half than at any previous time since the State has been stocked to capacity; yet in actual valuations it reached more than $1,500,000.00 divided among the five principal predacious species. . . . The damage by gray wolves in this state to livestock alone, and at prevailing figures, at the time operations by the Bureau were begun in 1915, should have been placed at half a million dollars in place of $300,000.00 as was the case.

In Arizona, Musgrave (1920) was less verbose: "we have the wolves down by at least 30%."

In October 1920 E. L. Pineau of the field hunter force assumed the duties of predatory animal inspector for New Mexico, and Charles F. Bliss, biological assistant, was made the executor of the predatory animal control program for the state. During 1921, 56 gray wolves, including 23 young, were reported taken in New Mexico (Bliss 1921) with another 37 in Arizona (Musgrave 1921).

During this period there was a movement in Hidalgo County, New Mexico to downplay bounties and advocate a "wolf proof" fence along the United States–Mexico border. Several letters from ranchers advocating a fence and praising the Bureau were sent to the predator animal inspector in Albuquerque at the end of January 1921 (Fig. 2.4). Although such fences were long known to be ineffective (Young 1944), the issue continued to be advocated from time to time.

Bliss had his own solution to the problem of wolves migrating into the United States from Sonora and Chihuahua. American ranchers in Chihuahua had hired their own hunters; he proposed that the Bureau select and oversee hunters who would work year-round in Chihuahua and Sonora. There was, however, no evidence that his suggestions were ever implemented.

While debate continued over methods of control, 13 adult males, 12 adult females, and 3 young were taken in New Mexico, and 58 wolves were reported destroyed in Arizona in 1921 and 1922 (Musgrave 1922). Eddy Anderson trapped 5 wolves that drifted into Hidalgo County from Mexico.

In efforts to keep hunters informed, Musgrave issued monthly newsletters (Fig. 2.5). These communications furnish good insight into the attitude that prevailed at the time.

Musgrave made a strong pitch to his men to expand their use of poison. Some of his men, particularly in lion areas, were reluctant to use this tool for fear of their dogs and also because such kills could not always be retrieved for credit—an important incentive. Despite their misgivings, approximately thirteen million acres

Predatory Animal Inspector
Albuquerque, New Mexico

Dear Sir:

There is little chance to estimate the losses in past years from lobo wolves over the lower division of the Diamond A Company holdings. Lots of calves and yearlings were killed each year, and the damage would run into thousands of dollars. Since your men have worked here many lobos were killed, until probably about ten wolves range in and out of their breeding grounds in Old Mexico. There have been 25 in the drift before. The original number and its increase has been decreased.

The constant drift from Old Mexico has caused us a loss of $25,000.00 annually. The only way to keep down the kills will be to have a man located here to catch the drift as it comes in. The international boundary ought to be fenced and the trouble could be handled then. Until this is done one man will have his hands full to keep down the heavy loss. We used to pay a $20.00 bounty a head on lobos for a good many years, but stopped it because it was abused. Lobo scalps from Arizona, Sonora and Chihuahua were often brought in claiming bounty. The bounty system has been a failure as a means of keeping down losses over this range.

There is no doubt that your system and work year after year has been a success and held down more than the drift and will handle the problems the best. With a fence along the boundary line your men could clean out the lobos in this section in a short time.

Hoping that you can keep a trapper in here and keep up the good work, I am.

Yours truly,
(Signed) Ben Robertson
Manager—Lower Division
Diamond A Ranch

Figure 2.4. Excerpts from letter from ranch manager advocating wolfproof fence

of Arizona grazing land were treated with poison in
1923. Of the 37 wolves reported taken in Arizona by
PARC hunters in 1922–1923, 14 were killed by poison.
Stockmen reported another 6 to 8 wolf carcasses on
their ranges, presumably poisoned. Undoubtedly, there
were others.

In fiscal year 1923, Eddy Anderson took one
Mexican wolf in Hidalgo County, New Mexico. W. C.
Echols was stationed in southern Hidalgo County for
the specific purpose of catching wolves as they came
across the border, before they could inflict damage in
New Mexico. The use of poison was encouraged there,
too, as reported by Pineau (1923):

> During July and August an effort was made to secure
> cooperation of ranchmen along the border of Mexico
> to exterminate wolves along the Mexico-New Mexico
> border. The Otero County division of the association
> reported taking three wolves and three wolf pups with
> Government poison in August and September. Cooper-
> ative operations concerning wolves gradually decreased
> leaving Federal and State hunters to continue the work.
> Complaints of damage to livestock, especially the
> larger species, have not been so numerous as hereto-
> fore, due to the large number of predatory animals killed
> on the more important ranges where drift and breeding
> have been in evidence. Hunter Echols took 13 wolves
> on the Mexico-New Mexico border. This accomplish-
> ment rates Mr. Echols high man on wolves, and also
> substantiates the claim that there is a steady drift of
> these animals from Mexico.

A total of 32 wolves was taken in 1923 in New Mexico
by government hunters, 30 trapped and 2 shot (Pineau
1923). This brought the two-state total to 69; using

PHOENIX, ARIZONA
October, 1922

HUNTERS' NEWS LETTER
ARIZONA DISTRICT.

The Hunters' News Letter is gotten out for the information of the hunters in order to convey news to them from other parts of the State, to show what each man is doing and to give general instructions from this office when necessary.

There has been some very creditable catches made this month but no one exceeded the speed limit by a great deal.

J. M. Wilson, of Fort Grant, caught four bear that had been killing cattle on the west end of the Graham Mountains and is given first place on the honor roll. However, I wish to mention now so that the men will take it under consideration in the future that we do not feel that bear are as great a credit to a hunter as the wolves and lions although sometimes they are just as destructive as either of the other two animals but they are much easier to get. Notwithstanding this we congratulate Mr. Wilson on his catch.

Fred Willis, who has become one of our veteran poisoners, deserves congratulations on getting an old renegade wolf in the vicinity of Nelson. This was a good piece of work as the wolf was very sly and covered a large range.

In a recent letter from the Washington office we were requested to save some bear galls, so I should like to have hunters save the gall of any bear that they get. Remove the gall bladder and hang it up in the shade until it dries, then ship it in to this office.

I have found it necessary to drop two men from the Service on account of their inability to keep up a good catch. This I hate to do but it is necessary unless a man can keep up to a certain standard.

J. M. Wilson, who has always worked on mountain lions and smaller predatory animals distinguished himself by catching two lobo wolves, one a female suckling young and the other a large male. That is the kind of work that counts. The man who can handle any situation that arises on the range is of great value to the Service and I wish to complement [sic] Mr. Wilson on his good work.

Phoenix, Arizona
December, 1925

December was not a good month for predatory animal work in the State of Arizona. There are two men on the list showing a no catch record. Several others have taken but very few animals, some of them are new men and we are finding it necessary to drop them from the Service and replace them with other men. If the animals are on your district to be gotten we feel that you should get them and I do not feel that it is necessary for any men to work any length of time without catching some predatory animals.

For the benefit of new men on the force I wish to state that we grade their catches in the following manner: One fox is one-half point, one coyote or one bobcat is one point, one bear is ten points, one lion 15 points, one wolf 15 points, and wild dogs are graded according to the damage they have been doing or the locality they are working in. Some of them are as bad as wolves, others are not. It is necessary to have fifteen points or one-half point per day for the time you work in order to get on the honor roll.

REMEMBER OUR SLOGAN, "BRING THEM IN REGARDLESS OF HOW."

	Respectfully submitted,
K. P. PICKRELL	M. E. MUSGRAVE
Assistant Inspector	Predatory Animal Inspector

Figure 2.5. Excerpts from newsletters sent to Arizona PARC hunters in 1922 and 1925

every device available, PARC appeared to be getting on top of the wolf at last.

That progress was being made was borne out in 1924 when 22 adult and 7 young wolves were destroyed in Arizona, and 34 (excluding 5 "hybrids") were taken in New Mexico. Except for 10 animals taken in Rio Arriba County, New Mexico and a few in northern Arizona, most of the 56 adult animals taken were in the border country, or at least below the Mogollon Rim. It was also about this time that Albert Pickens took the last wolf in the Black Mountain–Cooney Prairie area on George W. "Dub" Evans's ranch southwest of Magdalena (Pickens 1980).

After a brief absence from the state, Ligon returned to New Mexico as inspector in September 1923. He expressed his pleasure with the progress in his 1924 report:

> A survey of the wolf situation in the State indicates that these, the greatest cattle-killers, are no longer a real menace. During the year complaints were received of wolves depredating in various sections throughout the state; dead or wounded cattle or tracks of what were supposed to have been wolves furnishing the evidence. In some cases the inspectors were sure there were no wolves, while in others, depending on locality, there would be some question regarding foundation for reports. In more than seventy-five percent of the cases, investigation disclosed the fact that dog or coyotes and in some cases hybrids, wolfdogs were the offenders.
>
> At the close of the Fiscal Year there were perhaps a dozen adult wolves and hybrids in the State. None remain east of the Rio Grande. During the year thirty-nine wolves and hybrids were secured by salaried hunters of the service, nineteen of these having been taken on the Mexican border by one hunter.

Although Stoke's estimates were once again on the optimistic side, this time he was basically correct. The wolves' time had come. Thirty-one "wolves"* were taken the following year in Arizona, all by Charles Gillham. During this period 28 wolves were trapped, 4 were poisoned, and 2 were shot in New Mexico (Ligon 1925). Only 3 additional wolves were reported taken by ranchers across the state.

THE BORDER PATROL YEARS—1925 TO 1950

By 1925 the wolf had ceased to be a major predator in the southwest United States. Except for a few possible holdouts on the Fort Apache, San Carlos, and Jicarilla Apache Indian reservations, resident wolves had been effectively eliminated. Only Mexican wolves entering the border states from the Sierra Madres were cause for concern.

In his annual report for fiscal year 1925, Inspector Ligon (1925) discussed the wolf control situation in New Mexico:

> The passing of the wolf in New Mexico, as well as in other western states, is every year becoming more apparent. While eradication of this species has not been completed, it has so far advanced that very little complaint of stock killing, which has been shown with certainty as chargeable to wolves, has occurred in the state during the year. The "Lobo's" final exit from New Mexico has long been heralded. His stay, which has been far too long, seems fast drawing to a close.

---

*The biological identity of many claimed wolves is open to question. Everett Mercer and other district supervisors later challenged the authenticity of some of these reports.

So far as is known, no wolves are rearing young within the borders of the state this year. However, should it later be found that this happened, present plans of operations for the Fiscal Year 1926 preclude the possibility of a like occurrence next spring. Every resident wolf within the borders must be disposed of within the year; ample provision is to be made for guarding against infestation from Mexico; cooperative wolf work planned between the district leaders of Colorado and New Mexico should eliminate any remaining wolves now ranging in southern Colorado and New Mexico, while according to reports on conditions in Arizona, there seems little to fear from that source.

In his report on the Arizona district that year, Musgrave (1925) stated:

... at the end of the last fiscal year, we made the statement that there were six adult wolves left in the state. Our men caught four wolves that were indigenous to the state and six that drifted in from outside. [An additional] twenty-one wolves were taken along the border that were migrating north into the United States from Old Mexico.

Of the nearly fifteen hundred large predators (wolves, lions, bears and coyotes) destroyed in Arizona the following year, only 18 were wolves. Musgrave (1926) reported somewhat prematurely that "fiscal year 1926 has been a banner year ... this year marks the end of the lobo wolf for there are no more wolves left inside the borders of our state."

The 1926 annual report for Arizona included a letter from Henry Boice, manager of the Chiricahua Cattle Company along the Black River, traditional wolf range that only a few years earlier had been described as "great wolf country." Boice claimed "there are no indications of wolves drifting through our range . . . at the present time."

In fact, a few wolves did remain, and others would continue to drift into Arizona and New Mexico from Mexico for almost another five decades. These incursions could and did result in damage, but the strategy was to prevent these wanderers from reestablishing a resident population. This required stationing the best wolfers along the United States–Mexico border, to immediately respond to reports of wolf damage and remove offending animals as soon as possible. It was hoped that wolf work could be extended into Mexico and eventually reduce or eliminate that reservoir. These border patrols, difficult to justify on a cost-benefit basis, were designed as a preventive measure. As such they were unquestionably successful.

New Mexico

In his 1925 report, Ligon praised the work of PARC hunter W. C. Echols. Working near the border in Hidalgo County, New Mexico, Echols trapped 4 large wolves in one night in November. Ligon was so impressed with this man's "splendid work" that he included a letter from Echols:

These traps I covered early in the morning carrying with me a small light pole, spiked at the end for this purpose, and never dismounted from my horse unless [the] trap was sprung. The cover used was the largest piece of dry cow manure I could find. After sundown [the] stock had all gone out from water. I then rode this portion of trap line the second time, uncovering traps as

I had covered them. I must say I was fortunate, as the wolves did not come along until my scent was all gone from setting the traps.

On the night of November 8th, four wolves came into the small spring for water. . . . Three of them got caught in the first three traps. I regret that I did not have a Kodak to make pictures of them as all three were within fifty yards space on the trail and would have made an excellent picture. I placed these traps close together on trail for fear wolves would turn back or quit trail after first catch. The fourth wolf did quit trail and led back to another trail running north, and caught in the last set on this trail.

I wish to say at this point of my narrative, that after killing the three wolves I began looking for the tracks of the fourth wolf. After finding the tracks, I was following them, when I looked on about ¾ of a mile ahead and saw wolf in my trap. Upon getting near wolf, it pulled up the trap pin and a race followed for about one half mile to where I roped the wolf. As soon as the loop of the rope tightened around his neck, the wolf whirled and snapped the rope with one vicious bite. The wolf I then shot.

Echols's catches brought the tally for 1925 to 28 gray wolves trapped, 4 poisoned, and 2 shot in New Mexico (Ligon 1925). Three additional wolves were taken by non-PARC personnel. Besides the 18 wolves known taken in Hidalgo County, at least some taken in Grant and Catron counties may have been Mexican wolves. The 6 animals from Rio Arriba County on the Colorado border, probably in or near the Jicarilla Apache Indian Reservation, would have been among the last Inter-mountain wolves taken in the Southwest.

Echols made another notable catch in 1926, again in Hidalgo County. Of the 4 wolves he took in the county that year, one had a dog for a companion. The dog, which Echols caught first, wore a collar and name plate identifying its owner in Cochise County, Arizona. It was believed that the dog joined the wolf on raiding trips because the wolf was without a mate.

In addition to the 4 gray wolves caught in Hidalgo County, 3 were taken by government hunters in Rio Arriba County and 1 in Grant County (Pope 1926), while 4 gray wolves were taken by cooperators (Pope 1926). This was the lowest annual take of wolves by the PARC in Arizona since work began in 1915.

In August 1926, E. F. Pope hired Al Field to hunt wolves and lions on Field's ranch in the Peloncillo Mountains on the Arizona–New Mexico state line. This enabled Echols to work farther east along the Mexican border.

The main crossing point for wolves entering from Mexico was along the southern border of Hidalgo County between the Guadalupe and Peloncillo mountains and between the Peloncillo and Big Hatchet ranges. Most of the wolves Echols took were in these areas.

The service still hoped to station a man in Mexico and, if not, to construct the border fence. Ollie Glaze, a noted wolf hunter, had been employed by stockmen in Chihuahua to trap wolves on American ranches. With unsettled conditions in Mexico, Glaze planned to leave unless Pope could hire him to work for the PARC in Mexico south of Columbus and El Paso, Texas, where he could capture coyotes and wolves that might drift across the border. Glaze had destroyed "several hundred" wolves in Mexico and had been "very helpful" in keeping them from crossing the border (Pope 1926).

Nonetheless, it was the indefatigable Echols who continued to be the major barrier to wolves crossing the border into New Mexico. Throughout 1927 and early 1928 he wrote detailed accounts each month describing his efforts and methods (Echols 1927, 1928).

After hearing reports of wolves on the east side of the Animas Mountains, he established a camp at the northern end of the mountains, planning to work south to cut off the wolves and prevent them from entering farther into New Mexico.

In February 1927, Echols tended his trapline and waited:

> On the 23rd I succeeded in taking the worst one, or at any rate, the one I believe to be the hardest to catch, an old female with one foot missing. This wolf I caught at the spur tank about 15 miles north from Culberson Ranch. The same day I saw tracks of two more where they crossed the canyon on Adobe Creek near OK Ranch and on the following night the two came on across the range and I was told caught a calf near the Mexico line the same night.
>
> I am now preparing to place my traps in the most likely passways for them and await results, as I do not believe there is much chance of getting results by following them up. They cover 40 miles of country to my personal knowledge on the States side, and probably more in Mexico.

Echols found that the wolves continued to shift their range. Moving with them, he took his traps from near the Culberson Ranch and set them near the Spur Ranch where in March he caught one wolf and started on the trail of another:

David E. Brown

Because of their proximity to the Mexican border, the Animas Mountains in New Mexico's "panhandle" provided a natural travel route for lobos coming in from Mexico. The Animas range is a northern extension of the Sierra Madre.

On the 9th of the month, a large female wolf came up my trapline from the Spur toward OK Ranch, and located and went around every trap. On the following day, I rearranged, or re-set, every trap moving them some and fixed the places where I took them up back just as if the traps were still there, and on the 16th succeeded in taking this same wolf.

The male wolf came up Brushy Canyon and rolled on a set and the trap evidently got a hold on his side or back, as I found it about 100 yards from the place of setting, and the jaws were full of long wolf hair.

I then moved camp to the OK Ranch to hunt sign of the wolf, and succeeded in finding where he had crossed range near Gillespie Peak about 5 miles northeast of Adobe Ranch. However, it seems he is not going to locate near this point.

With good weather, Echols pursued his trapping in April and May. It was slow work, however, because of the rough, rocky country where tracks were impossible to find and because the wolf he was after had become trap-shy:

Twice during this time I saw only one track, and although I hunted all around, no other tracks were visible. When a wolf quits traveling trails, anyone familiar with them knows the job of taking one of this character. However, I did manage to get my wolf, which proved to be of somewhat freakish color. The fur has more of the color of a sloth than a wolf. The pelt and skull of the animal were saved for specimens. I hope they will be of as much interest to others as it is to me.

At this writing there is evidence of another *hard number*, but as long as they come, I shall catch 'em.

The old wolf that was shy about three toes came back, headed for the Land of Mañana . . . and started to go up Bear Canyon but upon reaching the first trap which had been sprung by a fox, he changed his mind. Right there he crossed the high ridge his last time and started up the head of Adobe Creek.

Upon reaching the first set on this trail, he made a very lucky jump and got over this set altogether, but was not so lucky at the second trap near cement tank for he stepped too short and got caught.

A few days later I saw tracks lower down crossing
Adobe Creek, but owing to high wind blowing and
tracks being almost invisible, I am not sure if it was a
wolf or a dog; however, it was very likely a dog as I
saw Mr. Timberlake's man, and he reports no sign, nor
could I find any sign later.

While Echols was working on the border, other government hunters took 21 wolves in New Mexico in fiscal
year 1927 (Gray 1927), and cooperators took 4 wolves
in Rio Arriba County.

In the fall of 1927 some wolves entered New Mexico
from Colorado, settling in the Tres Piedras country
where they took a large number of young cattle along
the Tusas River (Pickens 1980). It took Albert Pickens,
one of the PARC's top wolfers, his brother Homer, J. E.
Hawley and rancher Oscar Royal the better part of a
year to eliminate 7 wolves. Trapping was extremely
difficult because of the numerous coyotes in the area
and the wariness of the wolves (Hawley, personal communication). One wolf, Old Three Toes, one of the last
to be taken in northern New Mexico, was viewed years
later by its captors with admiration and regret at having
to trap it (Fig. 2.2; Pickens 1980, J. E. Hawley, personal
communication).

A. E. Gray (1927) discussed the year's take:

All of the wolves taken this year were taken close to
the borders of the State. This may indicate that none
exist in the interior of the State, and most of the
invaders have been picked up within a short time after
crossing into the State. We think that the practical way
to prevent the wolf from becoming re-established in the

J.E. Hawley

Oscar Royal and Old Three Toes, one of the last wolves taken in northern New Mexico. This animal weighed 109 pounds and was one of a small band of Intermountain wolves that came out of Colorado in 1927. It was caught in 1928.

State is to maintain a close watch of all known habitats, and to keep on all of our experienced wolf hunters in close proximity to these ranges. This scheme is applicable, except along the Mexican border, where we must maintain a hunter whose duties will be to patrol constantly the country through which the wolves travel when entering the State. The other wolf hunters will hunt coyotes and lions, except when it is necessary to work after wolves that are known to exist. We do not think that the numbers of wolves in the State demand attention other than this.

For hunter Echols, all his attention was on the wolves that ranged the border country in and near the Animas Mountains. Through October, November and December, despite his diligent pursuit, one wolf continued to elude his traps:

The wolf that visits the Animas Mountains only comes in at intervals, and does not make the same round at each visit following along the roughest part of the range. Therefore, it is very difficult to make any progress toward taking it. In addition to this, it has been very stormy and cattle have caused me a great deal of grief by springing all my traps. If I had not had the misfortune of having my set disturbed at the pine tree where I had one 150 bear trap and two 14's set in a trio, I am quite sure Mr. Wolf would have been caught this month. Of course, when he located the set, I had to move it down the canyon about a half mile and recently the cattle have taken possession of the canyon, so that I was forced to move my traps. Prospects for a catch are very unfavorable as very little sign can be found, and at present, stock is very numerous all over the high range.

After a heavy snow had melted and the ground was frozen, the wolf came over my entire trapline on Walnut Creek without a mishap. I could see his tracks at different places along the line where the sand had dried enough on the surface so that it did not freeze, and at one trap I could see where he stepped in the center of the trap.

Undaunted by the setbacks, Echols stayed on the trail of this particular wolf, and in January the offending animal was caught, but it escaped. Echols (1928) recounted the episode:

> On the 4th I found sign of him . . . however, there are so many cattle there, it would have been impossible to have kept a trap setting. I found no more sign of the wolf until I caught him on Walnut on the 28th. He was caught in the same trap that I accidently caught the big bear in last spring, and I suppose the bear had strained it just about to the breaking point. At any rate, the wolf had started off from a slope apparently running full speed. The hook drag caught a mahogany about 20 inches from the ground, one post was broken off of the trap, and one jaw of the trap was also broken. The trap had sprung back and landed in a tree some 3 feet from the ground, and I do not believe from the sign that it ever checked the wolf at all.

In February 1928 Echols's supervisor complimented his efforts:

> Echols did a splendid piece of work by taking two wolves and one lion in the Animas and Peloncillo ranges in lower Hidalgo County. One of the wolves taken, a male, has been ranging this country for the past 7 months. It had avoided Echols best efforts, and the taking of this animal is indeed a commendable piece of work. The female was taken at the same time, and again attempts of the wolves to become established within the State were broken up by prompt and efficient work (Gray 1928).

In addition to the two Mexican wolves that Echols took in Hidalgo County during the year, a private trapper reported taking one in Otero County and another in Catron County (Gray 1928).

During fiscal year 1929, Gray (1929) reported that Andy Campbell, who was newly assigned to the Animas area, took two wolves in Hidalgo County; one was a female carrying seven unborn pups. Other government hunters reported taking a wolf in Catron County and one in Grant County.

John C. Gatlin, who assumed leadership of the predatory animal control program from Gray, reported that Echols took 3 Mexican wolves in Hidalgo County in fiscal year 1930 (Gatlin 1930), the only wolves taken that year in New Mexico.

Seeing a need for a stepped-up trapping effort, Animas-area stockmen organized the Tank Mountain Wolf Club in August 1931. Members agreed to assess themselves a penny for each head of sheep and goats to hire another hunter. George M. Dunagan was employed, in cooperation with the Bureau, to conduct control operations on 162 sections of sheep and goat range.

Echols, however, was still the most successful wolf hunter. He took 3 Mexican wolves in Hidalgo County in 1931, all those taken in New Mexico in 1932, and 9 in the Animas Mountain area in 1933. Gatlin (1933) stated that the increased catch of 1933 was due to the discontinuance of wolf control in Mexico, and the subsequent increased number of wolves coming across the border.

Wolf taken in Hidalgo County,
New Mexico, in 1929.

Dunagan took a wolf in 1934 in the Animas area; one was also captured in Colfax County on the Colorado border by another government hunter (Gatlin 1934).

During fiscal year 1935, Echols took 6 Mexican wolves in southern Hidalgo County.

Mexican wolves were temporarily increasing in Mexico during 1936 and 1937, according to Gatlin (1937):

> Our wolf work was maintained in southern Hidalgo County in order to trap as many wolves as possible which migrate in from the Republic of Mexico. All reports indicate that wolves are materially increasing along the international line in the Republic of Mexico. American livestock interests are gradually moving out of Old Mexico, and there is a consequent decrease in the amount of wolf trapping being done in Old Mexico.

Nineteen wolves were taken from July 1, 1936 to June 30, 1937 in the state. Eighteen were trapped and 1 was poisoned (Gatlin 1937). Of these, at least 13 were adult Mexican wolves and 3 were pups, all taken in Hidalgo County, and probably all by Echols. About this time the last den of wolf pups was taken in New Mexico by government hunters about three miles south of Animas Peak (Bayne 1977).

Thirteen wolves were trapped in Hidalgo County from July 1, 1937 to June 30, 1938. Echols took 11 and Dunnagan took 2 (Gatlin 1938). Also, 6 additional wolves were reported taken in the state by various cooperators, but where they were taken is unknown.

Acting district agent C. E. Cates (1939) described the effectiveness, and costliness, of the wolf border patrol:

> The few wolves that would migrate into New Mexico were not given much opportunity to kill livestock as the Bureau's hunter, Mr. Echols, was consistently on the job. The few animals which we now take naturally makes the cost per animal quite high, but no doubt saves the Bureau and stockmen a great deal of money by preventing the animals from invading livestock ranges into the interior of the State.

In the same year Echols accounted for 8 Mexican wolves trapped (Cates 1939). The border patrol—Echols—succeeded in trapping only 3 wolves in Hidalgo County during fiscal 1940 (Cates 1940). During the next fiscal year only 2 wolves were trapped in southern Hidalgo County (Cates 1941).

Echols removed 10 wolves from Hidalgo County during fiscal years 1941 to 1943, of which 7 were taken by traps, 1 by strychnine, and 1 by a coyote-getter (Laney 1942–1943). One wolf was also reported taken by a cooperator.

After Echols's retirement, government hunter Arnold Bayne was transferred into the Animas Valley in the fall of 1943 to take up the work of wolf and lion control. He and his family moved to the OK Bar Ranch at Cloverdale and lived in Echols's old cabin. Bayne lived there a couple of years, then in several other places in the Animas Valley. On June 2, 1944 Bayne took his first wolf in the Animas Mountains with a coyote-getter. Bayne's records of his catches represent rare data on southwest wolves (Table 2.1).

TABLE 2.1

WEIGHT AND MEASUREMENT DATA
FROM 35 MEXICAN WOLVES TAKEN BY
ARNOLD BAYNE IN THE ANIMAS AND
PELONCILLO MOUNTAINS,
HIDALGO COUNTY, NM, 1945 TO 1966*

	Weight (Pounds)	Length† (Inches)	Tail (Inches)	Hind Foot‡ (Inches)
	MALES §			
Range	90–94 (3)	59–76 (16)	13–17 (16)	3–4.75 (16)
Mean	91.3	64.1	15.0	3.6
	FEMALES §			
Range	61–83 (3)	56–64 (11)	13–14.5 (11)	3–3.75 (10)
Mean	70.7	60.4	13.9	3.3

*Thirty taken in Newhouse traps; five with coyote getters
†Nose to tip of tail
‡Probably pad
§Sample size in parentheses

During his work in Hidalgo County Bayne did not use strychnine. Although he was certain that the poison killed wolves, he felt its effectiveness was reduced because wolves rarely returned to their kills. Dunagan, however, used strychnine for coyote control, from Lordsburg south to the border (Bayne 1977).

Most of Bayne's work was preventive, as the border patrol concept was designed to be, although numerous livestock losses sometimes occurred before a wolf could be caught. In one instance a wolf had killed more than twenty goats near Gillespie Mountain. After the rancher notified Bayne, he found the wolf trapped in Indian Creek.

Bayne took 3 wolves in traps in fiscal year 1945. In addition, cooperators took 14 wolves by strychnine in New Mexico (Laney 1945). In 1946 and 1947 Bayne took another 10 wolves, with 2 wolves taken with strychnine by cooperators (Laney 1946–1947). The apparent wolf increase in New Mexico was blamed on relaxed predator control in Mexico; Laney (1946) again made a plea for construction of a boundary fence.*

Bayne's catches continued to increase, with 9 Mexican wolves taken in 1948. Also, Alvin Dunnagan took 1 with strychnine during this period (Bayne 1977). The next year 3 wolves were trapped by Bayne in the Animas Mountains. In 1948 Compound 1080 was introduced into parts of New Mexico for coyote and wolf control (Laney 1948). It was not until 1950, however, that 1080 was placed in Hidalgo County (Laney 1950a).

Arizona

The history of wolf control in the second quarter of the century in Arizona was similar to New Mexico. After the lull of 1925 and 1926, 16 wolves were taken in Arizona by government hunters and cooperators during fiscal year 1927 (Musgrave 1927). Fourteen of these were in southern Arizona, close enough to the

---

*Given the digging ability of the wolf and the known failure of previous measures, the continued appeal of this proposal to professional PARC personnel is difficult to understand.

Mexican or New Mexican border to be considered transients. Reports and other catches indicated that wolves were also still present on the Apache reservations along Black River. Damage figures were not listed, but most of the wolves were caught soon after they crossed the border before they caused much damage. In 1928 Musgrave listed 1,643 major predators taken by the cooperative hunting force, and only five were wolves. However, more than ten million acres of grazing lands in Arizona were treated with poison (probably strychnine), and the number of wolves (and other "major" predators) killed may have been much higher.

Only 3 wolves were reported to have crossed into Arizona from Mexico, and 4 from New Mexico. No claims were made of wolf kills on livestock during the year. J. J. Tucker caught 4 wolves on the Double Circle range that had crossed into Arizona from New Mexico. The other wolf caught got into a trap set by Fred Ott in southern Arizona.

The following year, only 1 wolf of 43 claimed was caught by the PARC force (Musgrave 1929), but several hunters were assigned to investigate specific wolf reports. Musgrave personally visited the Guadalupe Canyon district east of Douglas, Arizona, where at least 1 wolf had been coming through from Mexico. A hunter, A. S. Field, was assigned to set traps on every pass in the Peloncillo Mountains and leave them set until the wolf was caught. In December Field found the wolf in one of his traps. Later, he caught a second wolf that got away, leaving two toes in the trap. Livestock losses to wolves were reported as negligible.

Between state and federal hunters, some eighteen hundred major predators were taken; only one was a wolf.

Seventeen wolves were destroyed in 1930 (Gilchrist 1930), 13 by federal hunters and 1 by a state hunter; another estimated 3 wolves were poisoned but the carcasses were never located. Such estimates were made when poison baits were picked up, and tracks indicated that wolves probably took them. Of the 14 wolf carcasses actually accounted for, 12 were poisoned and 2 were caught in steel traps. Eleven of the wolves were taken in Pima and Santa Cruz counties, within fifty miles of Mexico. These catches were all made by PARC hunter William Knibbe. Knibbe caught 5 wolves in one night.

Field took 2 wolves in Cochise County, and George Logan reported 1 in Coconino County where a wolf had not been taken since the early 1920s. Unfortunately, like most PARC catches, this animal was not verified by the PARC district office, leaving its authenticity open to question. The wolves caught by Knibbe and Field were taken soon after they crossed into the state, and damage to livestock was slight.

A pack of wolves was reported still inhabiting the Double Circle range along the Black River–Melay Gap area of the San Carlos Apache Indian Reservation, but PARC hunters were unable to catch any of them (Gilchrist 1930).

The annual report for 1931 lists "a few stray wolves . . . from Mexico" (Foster 1931). A wolf was finally caught along the Black River, and Knibbe trapped another old wolf that had taken a "heavy toll" of cattle on the U.S. side of the boundary. Hunter Eddy Anderson took another wolf in a blind set.

Foster, district supervisor for PARC in Arizona, claimed that taking the three wolves resulted in $1,800 worth of beef not being killed. His depredation tables showed that wolves killed twenty calves, one deer, and one antelope during 1931 (Foster 1931).

Considering the depressed national economy of these years, the following statements are significant:

> . . . although the cost-per-animal [caught] may seem somewhat high, consideration must be given the fact that our efforts are confined to the control of predators on those areas only where their depredations to livestock and game are of sufficient economic importance to justify their removal. . . . Present funds will not permit us to extend our operations to aid *all* who call for our assistance.

Nevertheless, Foster pledged to maintain the border patrol against marauding Mexican wolves on Arizona's southern and eastern borders.

In 1932 the PARC district supervisor somehow had been able to add another man to the border patrol. Total expenditures for salaries, including field men, were $33,043. Numbers of wild and domestic animals "known" to have been killed by predators during the year included forty-three calves, two chickens, four deer, and four steers killed by wolves. Eight wolves were recorded captured in Arizona during the year (Foster 1932).

Four wolves were again reported taken the following year (Foster 1933)—3 by federal men and 1 by a state hunter. Estimated predator-caused losses for the year were listed at $222,510, of which $45,836 was cattle.

Three wolves were destroyed in 1934 (Foster 1934). Two were caught by federal hunters, and 1 by a state man under PARC supervision. Total operating revenues were reduced to $20,588 ($17,469 for salaries), and only three predator hunters were in the field each month. For Foster's operations, these were lean times:

> Predatory animal work in Arizona faced the most crucial period in the history of the work. . . . Due to the shortage of funds . . . we could not maintain the air-tight patrol [against wolves] which we formerly kept on the border of Mexico (Foster 1934).

Operating funds for 1935 increased slightly, and Foster (1935) managed to have an average of four federal hunters in the field each month. The state of Arizona employed ten hunters under PARC supervision.

Seven wolves were caught—2 by federal men and 5 by the state trappers. One additional wolf was taken by a private cooperator with a trap furnished by the PARC.

In 1936 operating funds for the Arizona PARC district began to regain former levels, with help from state sources. Ten federal and ten state hunters were in the field, and 5 wolves were taken. Although no specific estimates of damages were given, Foster stated that there were

> Several reports of wolves drifting in across the border, but in each instance we have been successful in taking the wolves and keeping damage to a minimum (Foster 1936).

Five wolves were taken in steel traps during 1937 (Mercer 1937), all Mexican lobos. Two were caught in Cochise County in the Chiricahua and Peloncillo mountains, and 3 were trapped in Santa Cruz County in the Ruby-Baboquivari district, both traditional wolf runs. PARC field men specifically charged the wolves with killing eight calves and four deer.

In 1938 hunters took 2,344 predators of all classifications. Nonsupervised cooperators took another 397 bobcats and coyotes. Of 3 adult wolves caught in steel traps, 1 was a female taken in March with 6 unborn pups.

> Only three wolves were taken during the year. One of these . . . was taken on the Black River in Greenlee County [Double Circle range], while two were taken in the Peloncillo Mountains in the extreme southeastern part of the state in Cochise County . . . one pair of wolves running in the Baboquivari and Santa Rita Mountains near the Mexican border, killed about twenty head of cattle during the months of May and June. A hunter was detailed on June 1 . . . and had not been successful . . . at the close of the fiscal year (Mercer 1938).

As in New Mexico, Arizona experienced an increase in wolves from across the border in the 1930s. Correspondingly, wolf takes were up, with 8 wolves taken in 1939.

According to Everett Mercer:

> Wolves frequently entered the state from Mexico and were responsible for serious depredations on cattle . . . on one occasion it is known that eight of the animals [wolves] were operating in Santa Cruz and Pima counties at the same time. Reports indicated that these wolves *killed more than fifty head of cattle.* During the fourth quarter, a single pair of wolves . . . in Santa Cruz county . . . killed eighteen head of cattle and seriously injured fourteen more before they were trapped (Mercer 1939).

Wolves most frequently entered the state from Mexico along traditional wolf runs east and northwest of Nogales. Most came through the Huachuca–Canelo Hills–Parker Canyon area, but quite a few also came in through the Ruby–Altar–Baboquivari region. Two and occasionally three hunters were kept in the border country throughout the year to catch these invaders. Most wolves were reported to make a kill or two and quickly return to Mexico. Five wolves were trapped by state hunters in 1940 (Mercer 1940). One of these, that Mercer called "ole Pegleg," was taken in January near Arivaca. Local stockmen had accused this wolf of killing nineteen cattle in a year and a half.

Only one wolf was reported taken during 1941 (Mercer 1941). The single "wolf" was trapped in July near Green's Peak in Apache County. A number of wolf complaints from along the Mexican border were found to be based on depredations committed by coyotes and feral dogs. Verifiable reports of wolf depredations on cattle were virtually nonexistent that year.

In 1942, one young wolf, a two-year-old, was trapped near Limestone Point, about forty miles southwest of Winslow, Arizona. This was the last reported wolf from north of the Mogollon Rim and northern Arizona. It left no record of livestock damage. Seven wolves were taken in southern Arizona (Fig. 2.2).

Local residents belatedly reported in April that several lobos were at work near Fort Huachuca; Bill Casto, the PARC hunter assigned to investigate, soon discovered that a pair of wolves had denned and

raised a litter of pups on the western slopes of the
Huachuca Mountains. Casto trapped the male and
killed the pups—the last wolves known to have
been born in the southwest United States. The bitch
escaped—probably back into Mexico. There were
no cattle at the Fort, and the wolves had been subsisting principally on white-tailed deer, which were
locally abundant. Some apparent reluctance to invite
PARC hunters onto the military base prompted some
muscle-flexing in which the PARC forces perse-
vered. The "dangers" of letting such incidents get out
of hand, allowing wolves to reestablish a U.S. population, were resoundingly stated in the annual report
(Mercer 1942).

Five wolves were killed in Arizona during fiscal year
1943 (Mercer 1943). One wolf reportedly killed five
calves and a deer before it was captured. The other
wolves were probably not in the state long, at least no
livestock losses were attributed to them. Available sign
indicated that these 4 had been living on white-tailed
deer in the Huachuca and Chiricahua mountains.

Five more wolves were caught by the PARC during
1944 (Mercer 1944). One was said to have worked its
way up from the Mexican border as far north as the
Pinal Mountains in southern Gila County, where
stockmen claimed it killed two calves and several deer.
The PARC hunter assigned to the area trapped this wolf
soon after the complaints were received.

A pair of wolves killed at least three calves in
Cochise County. They too were quickly trapped.
Another wolf ranging in Pima and Santa Cruz coun-
ties was trapped in June after it had generated several

complaints. Another pair of wolves was reported ranging in the Baboquivaris, and several PARC hunters worked far into the Fort Apache Indian Reservation in search of a pack of wolves reported to be killing in that area; these wolves had not been located by the end of the fiscal year.

PARC hunters trapped another 5 wolves in Arizona during 1945 (Mercer 1945). One was captured in Cochise County, 3 in Pima County, and 1 on the San Carlos Reservation. One was an old wolf with blunted teeth and grayed muzzle, that reportedly had killed several calves in southern Pima and Santa Cruz counties. The other 4 were typical restless, young males that had not been in the state very long, and appeared to have been subsisting mostly on deer. A sixth wolf ranging in the Chiricahuas was trapped by a local stockman.

Wolf reports continued to come in from the Fort Apache Indian Reservation, sprawling, extremely rough country that was traditional wolf range. PARC personnel failed to find any workable sign of these wolves.

Despite reports of wolves along the border on several occasions in 1946, no serious livestock losses were reported, and only 3 wolves were reported taken by PARC hunters (Mercer 1946). One large wolf was killed by lethal bait in Cochise County during January. Sources reported thirty calves killed by wolves during the year—mostly on the Indian reservation.

Two wolves were caught in steel traps on the San Carlos Reservation in the spring, and 2 more were believed to be ranging on the Fort Apache Reservation.

On June 1 a PARC hunter investigated reports of wolves in the Baboquivaris. After three weeks of searching, the hunter learned that 2 wolves had been trapped earlier by a stockman in Bear Valley, south of Ruby, Arizona. Ranchers reported that several wolves entered the state from Mexico and committed depredations on livestock during 1947 (Mercer 1947). A lion hunter trapped a wolf in April and another in August in the Graham Mountains. A wolf was killed by a cyanide coyote-getter in the Santa Ritas during May. At the end of June 1947, two wolves were reported killing calves in the Arivaca district of southern Pima County.

Reports of wolves, with substantial evidence, continued to come in from both the Fort Apache and San Carlos Apache reservations, but the wolves were ranging over a wide area.

The 3 wolves taken during the year were in addition to 5,846 other "major" predators destroyed. Though not normally stock killers, bears now bore the brunt of a feverish predator control program. Forty-six bears were trapped, and fifty-eight were caught by dog packs during the year. In addition, forty-six mountain lions were taken.

Twelve wolves were reported taken in Arizona during the 1948 fiscal year (Mercer 1948)—all arrivals from Mexico. For the first time in many years, Arizona's $50 bounty was paid on 8 wolves. Four were taken by private hunters in Santa Cruz County, 2 in Pima County (Arivaca), 1 in Graham County, and 1 in Cochise County. PARC hunters accounted for the other 4 wolves taken. Hunter Douglas Fanning caught 2 of them—1 near Sonoita and the other in the Santa Rita Mountains.

Several wolves apparently entered the state during 1949 (Mercer 1949) and took a toll of livestock along the border country. One wolf was taken by a PARC-supervised hunter with a coyote-getter in the Santa Catalinas near Tucson in July. Four other wolves were taken by bounty hunters during the year.

A milemarker in wolf history in the Southwest was passed in 1950: "The fiscal year has passed without a single wolf being recorded by the cooperative hunting force. *This has never happened before*" (Mercer 1950).

Two wolves, however, had been reported ranging in western Graham County in December 1949. Another wolf was reported seen during the spring in the Huachuca Mountains, and a stockman on the east side of the Dragoon Mountains in Cochise County reported that a wolf killed a calf on his range on November 9. Wolves would return, but only in ones or twos; even these would become increasingly rare as the sources in Chihuahua and Sonora were depleted.

West Texas

Wolves had effectively been brought under control in Trans-Pecos Texas by the mid-1920s. Periodic incursions from Mexico also occurred in this region. Wolves undoubtedly were taken by bounty hunters, stockmen, and cooperating hunters, but no PARC district reports are available for west Texas. Scudday (1977) thought that between 1915 and 1945 the wolf kill may have averaged one or two a year with only occasional kills after 1945.

The only specific records pertaining to the border patrol in Texas that Scudday (1977) found were in the Brewster County Commissioner's Court records:

> It having been called to the attention of the court that the Federal Government was desirous of cooperating with Brewster County in exterminating Lobo Wolves, particularly in the southern part of Brewster Co. to the extent of paying a trapper $50.00 per month, and the ranchmen of the vicinity to pay $50.00 per month, and further that Mr. W. P. Williams had been selected as the trapper—it is therefore ordered by the court that the clerk be authorized to issue warrant to W. P. Williams for 50 dollars per month, payable monthly beginning March 15, 1926, and ending June 15, 1926, out of the general fund.

Thus, border patrol work in Texas was contracted out and not done by PARC personnel. In a follow-up of this entry, Milton Caroline, state supervisor for the U.S. Fish and Wildlife Service in San Antonio, found the following notation in the state's 1926 annual report:

> . . . reports reached this office that some lobo wolves were depredating the lower part of Brewster County. Upon investigating it was learned that originally these wolves came from Mexico. Three of the six wolves had been killed at the time the report reached me. Hunter W. P. Williams caught two of the three.

A photograph of a wolf that Williams caught near Terlingua appears in the July 1955 issue of the *Sheep and Goat Raiser* (Landon 1955). This wolf appears almost black in the photo.

Another Brewster County Court record shows the Texas penchant for maintaining a local control program:

> 14th October, 1929—The county was petitioned for and
> authorized for the employment of a . . . trapper and
> poisoner to help exterminate predatory animals in the
> southeastern Brewster County from Rosenfield south to
> the Rio Grande, and west to Dove Mountain.

The stockmen would pay one-half the cost and the state
and county would each pay one-quarter. The motion
passed. Wolves may or may not have been involved in
the predation complaints.

On March 31, 1934, an entry was made in the Pecos
County records:

> Recently Pecos County purchased a number of steel
> traps which were used in a wolf eradication program.
> The county, having no further use for such traps,
> Commissioner Pyle moved that these traps be sold at
> cost and the proceeds applied to set up as a bounty
> fund to be paid Ray Baumgardner for killing wolves
> [coyotes?] from his airplane.

The last and only "native" wolf of record since 1901 in
the Trans-Pecos was a *monstrabilis* taken by Nelson
Elliot in 1942 in Presidio County (Scudday 1972). The
next wolf recorded from west Texas was a female
baileyi killed in Jeff Davis County in 1944 (Scudday
1977). This was the first of that subspecies recorded on
the basis of actual measurements, although the wolves
taken in the late 1920s by W. P. Williams in the Big
Bend country were almost certainly that subspecies.
The two wolves taken in 1970 in the Trans-Pecos were
also assumed to be *baileyi,* and they were either
wanderers from Mexico or had been released. If they
were wanderers, it is puzzling what caused them to turn
up in west Texas far from recent travel routes and where

they would have come from in Mexico. Whatever the circumstancs of their arrival these were the last authenticated wolves taken in Texas.

Mexico

Except for references to the employment of wolf trappers by American ranchers in Chihuahua (Nunley 1977), actual accounts of wolf control in Mexico from 1925 to 1950 are lacking. Nonetheless, enough is known to make some general inferences. The 1920s heralded the sputtering end of Mexico's revolutionary period; the country's frontier northern border was to be settled by Mexicans as provided by the Constitution of 1917.

From 1934 to 1940, during Lazaro Cárdenas's presidency, many large estates in Mexico were broken up and small plots of land given to peasants. Many of these large ranchos in Chihuahua and Sonora had been owned or operated by Americans. The portioning of these lands and the generally poor economic conditions caused professional predator trappers, mostly gringos, to leave the country.

These measures undoubtedly resulted in a few years of reduced pressure against the wolf and led to concern about wolves along the border. The Cárdenas administration, however, also built schools, hospitals, and modern roads. Communication and transportation improved. Sawmills and farms were established in the virgin forests of the Sierra Madre. By 1940 many of the previously lightly grazed pastures of northeast Sonora and Chihuahua were showing signs of overuse (Shreve 1942, Leopold 1949, 1959).

With more small ranchers and farmers came increased conflict with the wolf. Poisoning and trapping
were stepped up, and the repetitious pattern continued—
introduction of livestock, destruction of game, increased
wolf depredation, and intensified control measures.
The difference now was that this was the final act: no
wilderness remained for the wolf in the Southwest. By
1950 the population of wolves in Mexico was dwindling
rapidly (Leopold 1959). The wolf's fate in the Southwest was to be hastened by the development of new
chemical predacides like Compound 1080 and sealed
by the *ejido* concept of land reform.

THE END OF THE LINE AND
THE ADVENT OF CHEMICAL PREDACIDES

The border patrol's basic strategy was to make the
swiftest possible response to each complaint. Each
wolf kill and nearby runway was painstakingly saturated
with steel traps along with a variety of bait scents. Each
steel trap, which required setting and "running," could
catch only one predator at a time. It was also common
practice to liberally distribute tablets of strychnine.
These "drop-baits" were nonselective and effective only
for a short time in cool weather. Chemical predacides,
on the other hand, could kill dozens of animals with no
more man-hour expenditures than setting a trap line.
However, since a poisoned animal would travel some
distance before dying, not all animals taken this way
were recovered. Thus, more wolves were probably
taken than were recorded. The PARC was continually
looking for a long-term, lethal predacide selective for
canines.

Compound 1080

The answer to their search seemed to be a rodenticide, Compound 1080, developed by the U.S. armed forces against rats in Burma, China, and Indochina. Chemically known as sodium monofluoroacetate, 1080 was so named because it was the one-thousand-eightieth in a series of formula modifications that the U.S. Fish and Wildlife Service had tried in readapting the compound for use as a predator control agent. It soon replaced another new predacide, thallium sulphate, because it was more lethal and selective for canids.

The original policy directives for use of 1080 in the field were issued by PARC director Albert M. Day on August 1, 1949. Detailed instructions and safety precautions were necessary for 1080, which was classified as "highly lethal." If carelessly handled, serious accidents could occur. Pets and other domestic animals were also in danger if they accidentally found a bait. Partly for these reasons, 1080 became quite controversial and its registration was eventually canceled by the U.S. Environmental Protection Agency in 1972.

Atzert (1971) described how 1080 was supposed to be used by the PARC to control coyotes in the West. (The wolf was no longer important.)

> . . . Baits are placed at established crossings and driftways having maximum use by coyotes in habitat having minimum use by most non-target carnivorous species. This practice, in conjunction with the Bureau policy of low density bait placement (normally no more than one per township) and the much smaller home ranges of most non-target carnivorous mammals, precludes a large percentage of the populations of these non-targets from even encountering the baits.

> ... Baits are placed as late in the fall as
> practicable, in keeping with effectiveness in controlling
> damage, and conditions of weather and travel. Baits are
> removed as early in the spring as weather and travel
> conditions will permit after allowing a suitable, but
> minimum time of exposure. To assure recovery, baits
> are securely fastened to immovable objects when set
> out in the fall and the location is described in writing—
> at least two persons must have firsthand knowledge of
> each location. Baits are disposed of by burning and
> burying or by deep burial.

In practice, preparation of the 1080 bait station usually involved shooting an old or wild horse, mule or burro. Just before killing the station animal, a Morton Meat Gun containing 1080 was readied. As the animal fell, it was deeply injected in several places while the carcass was still at normal body temperature. Capillary action circulated the lethal compound throughout the meat. If proper techniques were followed, all segments of the treated carcass were fatal to canines. Portions of the carcass, well-anchored to avoid scattering, were then distributed on a selected canine run.

Measured amounts of properly diluted Compound 1080 in animal carcass concentrations would kill a wolf, coyote, dog or fox, but were seldom fatal to nontarget species. Cattle and people were generally safe except under careless circumstances. Of course the recommended dosages were not always followed, particularly in private hands; in fact, the misuse (or intended use) of the compound is suspected of having killed some of the last grizzlies in Mexico. Nonetheless, its selectivity and effectiveness against coyotes made 1080 extremely popular with ranchmen and wildlife managers.

U.S. Fish and Wildlife Service

Preparing Compound 1080. The predacide is a powder that must be placed in solution to be injected into a freshly-slaughtered carcass. A Morton Meat Gun (on box lid in lower right) is used to inject the fluid.

An important drawback of 1080 was that even a lethal amount was slow-acting. As with other poisons, animals that consumed fatal doses died some distance from bait stations. Thus, determining actual numbers of wolves, coyotes, and other animals taken with this method was not possible.

PARC records unquestionably show that both thallium sulphate and 1080 were used to kill wolves in Mexico from 1950 through the late 1960s.

At the outset of the 1080 program, Laney (1950) stated:

> A cooperative wolf control demonstration in northern Mexico was carried on during the quarter. Assistant District Agent Crook and Mammal Control Agent Davis went into Mexico, and in cooperation with the Pan American Sanitary Bureau and the Mexican Government, demonstrated to American ranchers in the Casas Grandes area wolf control methods. Three wolves were taken and their report indicated that wolves are abundant a short distance in Mexico, south of the International Boundary.

Later, Laney (1958) reported on the effectiveness of 1080 as a wolf control tool in Mexico:

> At the 1950 demonstration, wolf populations were extremely heavy throughout the mountain country worked, and reports by stockmen and by Dr. Bernardo Villa who was present at the 1955 demonstrations indicate that a heavy population of the wolf existed in some of the demonstration areas worked. The 1958 demonstration covered a large portion of country tested with "1080" in 1950 and 1955, and observations lead me to believe that complete control of the wolf has been obtained and has existed for a 3 to 8 year period.
> Observation is attained from the reports of reliable stockmen and personal inspection of the known wolf habitat in 1950 and again in 1958. Mr. Alberto Verele, Pat Keenan, Ted Farnsworth, Lee Finn, Martin Jeffers, Otis Jeffers, Alberto Whitten, and Alvin Whitten said they had not had any livestock losses from wolf since the first "1080" was put into operation,

and that very little wolf sign had been noted in the past several years. Three separate wolf tracks were noted in the Gavilan River area during the 1958 demonstration. The New Mexico Branch of Animal Control has not taken a wolf along the International Border since 1952. Therefore, the Border stockmen in New Mexico have benefited considerably from the demonstrations given in Mexico.

Bayne (1977) considered the introduction of 1080 into Hidalgo County, New Mexico in 1950 an important element in the elimination of wolves in that state. Nonetheless, Gish (1978) thought that perhaps an even more decisive tool against the last migrant wolves in Arizona and adjacent Mexico was the cyanide gun or coyote-getter, brand-named "The Humane Coyote Getter."

The Coyote-Getter

This tool was specifically developed for coyotes and foxes, but when placed along trails or established runways, was used to take wolves also. A good description of its use is given by Anderson (1969):

It is a mechanical device which expels sodium cyanide and consists of a shell holder wrapped with fur, cloth, wool, or steel wool; a firing unit; a 38 cal. shell containing the sodium cyanide; and a 5–7 inch hollow stake. The stake is driven into the ground, the firing unit is cocked and placed in the stake and the shell holder containing the cyanide shell is screwed onto the firing unit. A fetid bait, usually made of fish, brains, or blood, is carefully spread on the shell holder. An animal attracted by the bait will try to pick up the baited shell holder. The cartridge fires when the animal pulls up on the shell holder and the cyanide is blown into the animal's mouth.

The animal pulling the coyote-getter lapses into a cyanide-induced coma in twelve to fifteen seconds and dies shortly (C. Carley, personal communication). In simplest terms, the "getter" was a short-barreled cyanide gun fired by a .38 caliber primer with a figure 4 triggering mechanism. In later devices the firing mechanism was spring-loaded. These getters, developed by a PARC trapper, are known as M-44s. The "M" stands for mechanical and the "44" relates to the fact that the plastic case containing the cyanide is .44 caliber.

As described by Gish (1978), and used in Arizona, getters were placed in clusters of about a dozen around a bait station. More often they were used singly along trails, scent posts, and near baits (C. Carley, personal communication). They were effective against such predators as foxes, coyotes, wolves, and bears, but cats presented special problems because they tended to pull at the getters with their paws rather than with their teeth.

Success

With the beginning of the 1950s, the wolf campaign was waning in the Southwest. Trapping and poisoning, combined with diligence, had paid off.

Only 2 wolves were trapped by the PARC during fiscal year 1950—both in Hidalgo County, New Mexico by Bayne. Four Mexican wolves were taken in Hidalgo County in 1951 (Laney 1951), 3 by Bayne and another claimed by Alvin Dunnagan. At least one Mexican wolf was taken by 1080 in Mexico as part of a cooperative demonstration by the Pan-American Sanitary Bureau.

Two wolves, reported to have killed twelve head of cattle in Arizona (Mercer 1951), were caught in August 1950. There were a few other reports of wolves during the year, but no additional livestock losses were claimed. Another 2 Mexican wolves were trapped by Bayne in 1952 in Hidalgo County, and 2 wolves were reported taken in Arizona that year (Mercer 1952), 1 of them in the Galiuro Mountains on April 3. A wolf was also reported to have made a kill (prey unidentified) in the nearby Pinaleño Mountains in June.

No wolves were reported by the PARC from either state in 1953, although a private trapper claimed the $50 Arizona bounty for an animal taken in the Pinaleño Mountains. For comparison with early and depression-year funding levels, the total PARC operating budget in Arizona for 1953 was $70,894.

Again in 1954 and 1955, no wolves were reported taken by the now well-equipped PARC personnel in the southwest United States. Mercer reported in 1955 that only two wolves crossed the border. No bounties were paid and no livestock damage was reported.

During this period, 1080 was very much in use in Mexico, as indicated by Laney (1955):

> For the second consecutive year, we report no wolves taken in New Mexico. This indicates that the "1080" Control program initiated in Mexico, and which was participated in again this year by Cliff Pressnall by a visit to that control area, is bearing fruit. We are informed by stockmen from south of the border, that livestock losses which used to run as high as fifty percent within a year have been materially reduced. I am sure that this is a program that has generated good will for our country from the Mexican stockmen.

Professional hunter Louis C. Cox displays the array
of equipment issued to predator and rodent control
personnel of the U.S. Fish and Wildlife Service.
These modern tools of the trade are in sharp contrast to earlier PARC hunters' gear.

By 1956 wolf reports were more frequent than wolves. Often these reports turned out to be large dogs or other predators. In fact, those people who actually knew wolves were, like the wolves themselves, passing from the scene. Great prestige was attached to taking a wolf— particularly the *last wolf*, and a number of animals were falsely claimed as wolves. Others were never checked by experienced wolf hunters or district superintendents. Although some wolves reported before 1950 were also undoubtedly dogs, unverified animals taken after 1950 must be viewed with cautious skepticism. "Wolves" reported taken far from the Mexican border and outside the Apache Indian reservations were almost certainly misidentified.

During 1955 and 1956 a wolf was reported to have fed from a 1080 station in Cochise County, Arizona; and on the night of December 15, 1955 PARC agent Harvey C. Day reported a wolf howl in the Gu Vo district in the southwestern corner of the Papago Indian Reservation where Indians had reported wolves killing cattle. George Peterson, the game ranger at Nogales, said he saw a wolf feeding on a freshly killed calf near Arivaca.

The only "wolf" taken by PARC personnel in New Mexico in 1956 was in Chaves County (Laney 1956). Arnold Bayne started concentrating his efforts in Hidalgo County on coyotes. The border patrol days were over.

Reports of migrant Mexican wolves along the border country persisted, and in 1957 a cowboy said he saw a wolf, and a deer kill was found on the Dubois Ranch in the Winchester Mountains in Graham County (Mercer 1957). Another apparent wolf-killed deer was found on the nearby Dee Jernigan Ranch. A cowboy on the

Cane Ranch in the Mule Mountains in Cochise County
rode up on a pair of wolves that had just killed a calf.
He believed his shots hit one of the wolves.

The next wolf was taken in January 1958 by Bayne
in New Mexico's Guadalupe Canyon. Two wolves
were then killed in Arizona by cyanide-loaded getters—
one in July near Elgin, the other near Redington between
the Catalina and Galiuro mountains. No other wolf or
damage reports were received during the year, and no
wolf bounties were paid (Mercer 1958).

PARC forces took no wolves in 1959, and no wolf
bounties were paid. One male wolf, with perhaps some
dog ancestry, was trapped alive by Raymundo Topas
in Peck Canyon in Santa Cruz County, Arizona. The
"wolf," the animal described in the beginning of this
book, was donated to the Arizona-Sonora Desert
Museum.

On February 5, 1960 a wolf was reported killed by a
getter northwest of the Nogales airport near the
Arizona-Sonora line. Then, in March 1960, PARC
hunter Russell Culbreath trapped a large male on the
Grasshopper District of the Fort Apache Indian Reservation. This was the last authenticated wolf taken by
the PARC in Arizona.

On April 23, 1960, Arnold Bayne took another wolf
in Hidalgo County, New Mexico, this time in Adobe
Canyon.

The next year a wolf was reported killed by a coyote-
getter on the Vaca Ranch in Red Rock Canyon in Santa
Cruz County, Arizona (Mercer 1961). The Arizona
Livestock Sanitary Board paid a $75 bounty for a wolf
trapped on the Schilling Ranch north of Willcox,

Wolf trapped by PARC hunter Russell Culbreath on the Fort Apache Indian Reservation near Grasshopper, Arizona, in March 1960. The wolf weighed 70 pounds, was 30 inches high at the shoulder, and 5 feet 4 inches from nose to tail.

Arizona. Schilling reported that the wolf had killed three calves before being caught. No other wolves were reported taken in Arizona for more than a decade.

In 1966 Arnold Bayne took his last wolf, a male, in Pine Canyon in Hidalgo County, New Mexico (Table 2.1). During 1966 and 1967 Bayne received word from ranchers of wolf carcasses they had found in southern

Hidalgo County, probably a result of 1080 or coyote-getters (Bayne 1977). These included two near Cloverdale, one in Guadalupe Pass, one in San Luis Pass, and one in Whitewater Canyon. The last wolf carcass found in New Mexico was reported in October 1970, by Bayne (1977) from the Peloncillo Mountains.

And so the wolf might have come to an ignominious end in the southwest United States, if it were not for the 2 wolves of unknown origin taken that year in southwest Texas—the only (and last) authenticated wolves from that state in more than twenty-five years. The first, a 2½-year-old male, was taken by a deer hunter in the Cathedral Mountains in Brewster County on December 5, 1970. The other, also a male, had been dead several days when found in a trap on December 28 near where Brewster, Terrell and Pecos counties meet (Scudday 1972).

No epitaph for the wolf in the southwest United States could be written, however, without mentioning the Aravaipa wolf in Arizona. Reports of a wolf's kills and tracks along the old wolf run in the Mule, Dragoon and Galiuro mountains west of Sulphur Springs Valley surfaced in the mid-1970s. A portion of the wolf's haunts in the north end of the valley at the head of Aravaipa Canyon had been acquired by a private group, Defenders of Wildlife. With the U.S. government's declaration of the Mexican wolf as an endangered species in 1976, controversy developed. Despite the possibility that this wolf was a wandering male, or even a release into the canyon, some people believed this animal might offer a chance for the Mexican wolf to stage a comeback and be saved from extinction. Wolf life history, and southwest tradition, dictated otherwise. The "wolf" was "quietly" taken by a private trapper for a reputed bounty of $500 put up by local stockmen. U.S. Fish and Wildlife Service photographs of the skull allegedly from the Aravaipa wolf indicate that the animal was a true wolf. If so, it is likely the last wolf taken in the U.S. half of the Southwest.

The quarter century from 1950 to 1975 was also not kind to the wolf in Mexico. The use of Compound 1080 and other poisons more than compensated for any reduction in professional American wolf trappers. Moreover, increased land use in northern Mexico was hemming in the wolf. The flourishing of ejidos, bringing resettlement of numerous, unskilled urban dwellers in remote rural areas, further decreased the already scarce game and increased conflict with wolves. By 1970 relatively few areas remained in northern Mexico that were not altered by human encroachment.

That the animals' reduction was real is attested to by the slowing, and finally absence, of wandering wolves along the United States–Mexico border. More than fifty years of persistent effort had succeeded.

We reached the old wolf in time to watch a fierce green fire dying in her eyes. I realized then and have known ever since, that there was something new to me in those eyes—something known only to her and to the mountain. I was young then, and full of trigger itch; I thought that because fewer wolves meant more deer, that no wolves would mean hunter's paradise. But after seeing the green fire die, I sensed that neither the wolf nor the mountain agreed with such a view.

Aldo Leopold, 1944

3

Life History

IT MIGHT SEEM ODD to find this section so late in the reading because life history studies are normally the prelude to the understanding and management of a species. This is not so with southwest wolves. No life history studies of a scientific nature have been conducted. The animal's hunting techniques for native prey were never documented, nor were its habits and social organization. Data from this region have, of necessity, been limited to the notes of wolf hunters working with depredating animals subject to stress. Consequently, some reported behavior may be atypical and uncharacteristic.

This does not mean that good life history information is totally lacking. Data obtained from wolf studies in other regions, such as those by Murie (1944), Burkholder (1959), Mech (1966, 1977), Pimlott (1969), Kolenosky (1972) and others, are in some ways relevant to the Southwest. Also, the wolf hunters were good

observers. Their knowledge of wolves and their habits
was an integral part of their job. Because of them, we do
know something about southwestern wolves. The
following information on wolf reproduction, behavior,
and social organization was gleaned primarily from
Bailey (1931), Young and Goldman (1944), Bayne
(1977), and McBride (1980).

PHYSICAL ATTRIBUTES

Southwestern wolves have the general appearance of
an oversize coyote. They tend to be attractively colored
animals, with some black and dark gray, brown, cin-
namon, and buff over light underparts. McBride (1980)
appropriately describes them as having an impressive
head with a short, thick muzzle and a large nose pad.
Their deep chest contours, thick necks, heavy fore-
quarters, and long forelegs give them a heavier
appearance in the shoulders than in the hindquarters.
The tail is generally dark-tipped. A long mane, or
hackles, is raised when the animal assumes a threat
posture.

Coat color varies with the season and the individual—even within the same litter. Although southwestern wolves tend to be dark (Goldman 1944),
some animals are nearly white. Others have a distinctly
tawny pelage, and some are so dark as to appear almost
black. McBride (1980) found a difference in color
between geographic populations. Wolves from
Chihuahua tend to be grizzled on the back and flanks,
whereas these parts are more tawny or brindled on
wolves from southern Durango.

Wolf portrait taken at the Arizona-Sonora Desert Museum. This wolf is one of the male litter-mates from a female trapped by Roy T. McBride in Mexico.

Neil B. Carmony

Wolves are sexually dimorphic: the males are measurably larger than the females. According to Goldman (1944), southwestern wolves are small to medium size, the Mexican race, *baileyi*, being one of the smallest North American subspecies. Adult southwestern wolves range from 4½ to more than 5½ feet long, including the 14- to 17-inch tail. Height at the shoulders ranges from 28½ to 31½ inches.

Since most wolf trappers preferred that their catches be recorded on the large side, even recorded weights must be viewed with caution. Gish (1978) relates an illustrative incident:

> When he became Arizona District Agent for the PARC in 1937, Everett M. Mercer was prodded by Dr. Charles T. Vorhies, biology professor at the University of Arizona, into checking the true weights of wolves taken by government hunters.
>
> Mercer sent out a circular to all PARC fieldmen in the district, instructing them to get accurate weights on each wolf caught. Soon after Mercer's directive, a schoolboy trapping coyotes 2 miles southeast of Williams, Arizona, caught a 2-year-old male wolf that weighed 58 pounds (Mercer 1966). A few weeks after that incident, veteran trapper John Ehn caught one male and one female wolf in the Santa Rita Mountains that he reported to have weighed 120 and 115 pounds. Mercer left the Phoenix office and was in Ehn's camp in the Santa Ritas before nightfall.
>
> Ehn swore that he had weighed the wolves according to Mercer's instruction on commercial scales in Patagonia, and that Bob Bagier, Arizona Game Ranger, George Peterson, and a man by the name of Gatlin on whose range the wolves were caught, witnessed the weighing.
>
> "John," Mercer grated, "how much do you weigh?"
>
> "About a 148."
>
> "O.K., you and I are going into Patagonia first thing in the morning. You are going to weigh yourself on those same scales. There aren't many wolves in this state that weigh much more than half of those you reported, but if you show up on those Patagonia scales weighing about 300 pounds, then I'll have to believe everything you reported about those 2 wolves."
>
> Ehn admitted that he hadn't actually weighed the two wolves—only guessed at the weights.

Arizona District PARC records show that soon after
the above incident, Ehn reported catching another wolf
that weighed 62 pounds. Later, Ehn caught another
huge old "Sonora wolf"—a male that weighed 74
pounds.

Particularly valuable, therefore, are the actual weights
of intact and eviscerated wolves taken by McBride
(Table 3.1). Allowing for an approximate weight loss of
20 percent for eviscerated carcasses, these data show an

TABLE 3.1

WEIGHTS OF ADULT MEXICAN GRAY WOLVES
FROM CHIHUAHUA AND DURANGO, MEXICO

Location	No. of Wolves and Sex	Weight (in pounds)	Mean
Chihuahua	6-Males	86*, 75, 91*, 70, 79, 80*	80
	4-Females	68, 71, 74, 64	69
Durango	6-Males	68*, 72, 79, 68, 77, 89*	76
	12-Females	62, 55, 68, 68*, 59, 63, 66, 58*, 54, 71, 59*, 67	62.5

Source: McBride (1980)
*Wolves with viscera intact; all other weights represent eviscerated
carcasses.

average weight of 89 pounds for adult male Mexican wolves and 77 pounds for adult females. His range of 68 to 99 pounds for males and 54 to 93 pounds for females agrees with the 66- to 99-pound range given by Leopold (1959) and recorded elsewhere (Young and Goldman 1944). These figures lend little credence to reports of southwest wolves weighing more than one hundred pounds.*

Even the smallest wolf is, nonetheless, substantially larger than the biggest coyote; a large male coyote in the Southwest may reach 35 pounds. The physiognomy and coloration of these two animals is similar, however, and unless one has seen a wolf in comparison, field identification may be difficult. The wolf's heavier build, wider face, and smaller, erect ears in relation to head size cannot be reliably used to differentiate the two by those unfamiliar with both species. The reported tendency of coyotes to carry their tails at a downward angle is also an uncertain means of identification. Tracks, however, can be a positive sign. The large forefeet of the wolf make tracks from 2¾ inches to more than 4 inches across—considerably larger than any coyote.

Differentiation between wolves and some dogs can also be difficult—even in hand. Wolves tend to have a fuller mane, fluffier tail, and longer muzzle than dogs (Mech 1970). The distinctive wide tufts of hair that grow out and down from the ears are perhaps the wolf's most diagnostic feature, along with a supracaudal gland

---

*Some exceptions have occurred among the Plains and Intermountain wolves. Gish (1978) cites a wolf taken in 1909 in southwestern Colorado that was reported to have weighed 125 pounds.

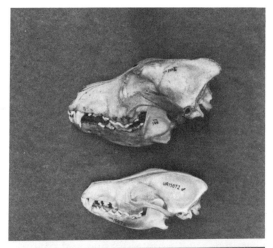

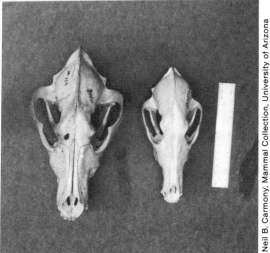

Skull of a male Mexican wolf killed in Pima County, Arizona in 1930 compared to that of an adult coyote taken near Marana, Arizona in October 1965. Unlike other parts of the country, in the Southwest the size difference between coyotes and wolves is great, leaving no room for misidentification.

above the base of the tail. Both of these are absent in dogs. According to Dr. E. Lendell Cockrum, University of Arizona, wolf hairs are distinct from most dog hairs when seen under a microscope (personal communication). Iljin (1941: 386) found that the two species could be separated on the basis of the orbital angle and other skull measurements. Lower tooth row alignment, curve of ascending ramus of the lower jaw, projection of the hard palate, shape and size of auditory bullae, and placement of the brain case have been found better and easier-to-use indicators (C. Carley, personal communication).

Gish (1978) and McBride (1980) state that wolf tracks can be distinguished from most dog and coyote tracks under most circumstances. Wolf tracks, besides being larger, are longer and narrower than those of a dog. The wolf's toes point straight ahead, but on a dog the two outside toes generally point slightly out from the heel pad (Fig. 3.1). Wolves also tend to run up on their toes with the center two pads' claw prints close together. Wolves' heel pads are also usually larger than those of a dog of similar size, and the toes are not spread as widely apart. Reading sign is an art, and although at times even the most proficient hunter might be fooled by individual tracks, the presence of wolves can safely be substantiated when other sign such as scent posts, scats (large and black), and kills are used to verify suspected tracks.

The wolf's massive skull supports a set of jaws and teeth of legendary strength. One of the wolf's most outstanding physical attributes is its biting power, enabling it to bite through a steer's hide and jerk out

Courtesy of the Will C. Barnes Collection, Arizona Historical Society

January catch of U.S. Forest Service hunter T.B. Bledsaw (right?) from the Kaibab National Forest around 1914. The large, light-colored wolf skin is conspicuous when compared to the coyote pelts surrounding it.

large chunks of meat. According to McBride (1980), wolves accomplish other incredible feats with their jaws such as biting off the trigger and pan of large traps. While holding wolves captive, McBride found it difficult to keep a suitable watering pan available. Wolves

Originally thought to be a Plains wolf (*Canis lupus nubilis*), a more thorough examination showed this animal to be a feral german shepherd–type dog. The dog was taken by tribal hunter Perry Garnenez on the Navajo Indian Reservation in February 1963. Note the absence of a mane on the animal.

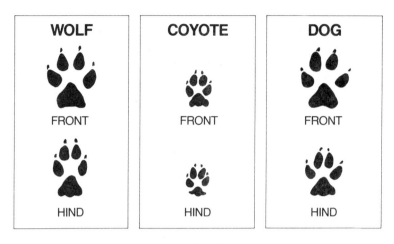

Figure 3.1. Comparison of wolf, coyote, and dog tracks

would completely destroy galvanized buckets and enamel pots and pans. To keep them from puncturing their food vessels, he buried cast iron skillets to ground level. How they can grind and bite on the chains that hold them without breaking their teeth is hard to imagine, but little damage was evident, even on wolves that had been chained more than a month.

Sense of Smell

Wolves use their keen sense of smell for defense and to find food, as well as to communicate with each other. An incident that demonstrates the wolf's acute sense of smell occurred in Sonora, Mexico and was recorded by McBride (1980). While trapping wolves on a cattle ranch one fall in the early 1960s, he used urine and

scats from a captive wolf as scent baits. After finishing
the job in December, he moved his traps. Five months
later he was called back to the same ranch because
another wolf had arrived. This wolf had visited three of
the old trap sites and apparently had smelled the bait
even though wind, rain, and sun had ample time to
erase the scent.

Another interesting observation by McBride occurred
southeast of Casas Grandes, Chihuahua where two
wolves were being held captive on a large cattle ranch.
These wolves were found as pups and were perhaps
two years old when McBride first saw them. Their diet
consisted of corn tortillas and beans, and they were not
given much of either. McBride began to feed them
animals that were accidentally caught in his traps—
coyotes, coatimundis, bobcats, and javelina—which
the wolves heartily consumed. These two wolves evidently began to recognize McBride from the other cowboys and fence builders constantly going to and from
ranch headquarters where the wolves were chained.
The cowboys told McBride that long before he would
arrive in the afternoon, the wolves would begin to pace
excitedly. After perhaps twenty minutes, the ranch
dogs would also detect his approach and begin to bark.
On every occasion the wolves detected McBride's
arrival long before the dogs did. Because he sometimes
brought food for the wolves, they displayed more
excitement than the dogs, but reacted whether or not he
was carrying any food on his saddle.

When McBride returned after a six-month absence
from the ranch, the wolves obviously remembered him.
The cowboys were impressed by the wolves' renewal of
tail-wagging and pacing and apparently excellent
memories.

Voice

The variations of the characteristic wolf howl have been described well by Young and Goldman (1944). They also noted a number of other barks, whines, and snarls given on particular occasions. McBride states that trapped wolves have a short, deeply pitched baying bark and can growl deeply. However, the most frequently heard noise is the long howling which serves to announce their presence and reunite them when they become separated. Once heard, it is never forgotten.

McBride (1980) once timed a continuous howl that lasted thirteen seconds. He found that howls vary little in pitch from beginning to end and are of relatively constant volume. Howls from deep rocky canyons are extremely loud and often have a ventriloquistic effect. Wolves are particularly prone to howling during the breeding season in late fall and early winter. At this time they are often reported near ranch houses where dogs are present.

The reaction of dogs is often comical. They have a deep respect or possibly fear of wolves, and either bark excitedly when wolves are howling or try to hide under a house. McBride reported that his hounds took little interest in captive wolves, but would return the howling of distant wolves with similar howls, a sound he never heard them make under other circumstances. He found that coyotes generally responded to wolf howls by barking and howling themselves, but that the opposite was not true when the coyotes howled first.

The howling of wild wolves is one of the most exciting wilderness sounds a human can experience; unfortunately, it is increasingly rare in Mexico and only a memory in the rest of the Southwest.

BEHAVIOR AND HABITS

Without systematic studies of wolf behavior in the Southwest, we are heavily indebted to the wolf hunters who recorded their observations and reminiscences. Again, foremost among them is McBride (1980), who described a number of wolf behavior patterns and reactions. He found that some trapped animals, when approached:

> . . . lunged wildly at the traps in an effort to escape. Others sulked or "cowered" and many barked and howled and reared forward in an aggressive manner, baring their teeth, raising their hackles and growling deeply. Several wolves lay still in the traps with very little evidence of a struggle to escape. Those with an aggressive attitude held their tails stiffly, either straight out behind their backs or in a vertical position and wagged them slowly from side to side. A high percentage of Mexican wolves were defiant, and difficult to take from a trap alive. Also, adult wolves were difficult to keep alive in captivity; many refused to eat or drink.

McBride (1980) also documented some remarkable displays of the innate wildness of wolves, despite their captivity. In one instance he witnessed a fight between an emaciated female wolf that had been chained nearly all her life and one of the ranch dogs:

> She was approximately three years old when I saw her and had been fed a sparse diet of leftover tortillas and beans. . . . Her head and feet were normal size, but her body was so underdeveloped that her front legs rubbed together. Her canines had been clipped off and she

appeared to be in no condition for a fight. There was on this same ranch a female German Shepherd. . . . One morning while I was saddling up, the German Shepherd for some reason jumped on the chained wolf. The little wolf at best couldn't have weighed 45 pounds and the German Shepherd forced her to the ground immediately and I thought she would easily kill the wolf. Since it was such an unfair fight, I tried to intervene, but the cowboys all insisted they be left alone. A great deal of blood began to appear on both animals and it soon became apparent that the wolf was disabling the dog by powerful bites with her jaw teeth on the dog's upper forelegs. When the cowboys saw that "Perla" was losing and in fact couldn't get loose, they roped the dog and drew her from the fight.

The wolf leaped up apparently unhurt and began to run excitedly to the length of her chain. When I returned in the afternoon, I found the wolf still very excited and the dog severely crippled in both front legs. I worked on this ranch several months and the dog had not recovered when I left.

Signposts

Wolves, like coyotes, make long scratches in the dirt, usually along frequently traveled canyon bottoms, low gaps in mountains and on the forested edges of mountain valleys. The scratches are made after urination by kicking with the hind legs and pulling backwards with the forelegs. If the scratch is in soft soil, deep toenail marks are usually evident. These three-foot-long marks, easily identified, were excellent places to set traps since all wolves in an area were attracted to those sites. Both sexes make "sign" but they are more often made by males, particularly during the mid-winter breeding season. Sometimes urine is sprayed on a vertical object, such as a prominent clump of grass, a low bush, or occasionally large tree trunks. Wolves also defecate on the sides of rocks and on the tops of low-lying bushes. They respond to wolf droppings along a trail by urinating on or near them and making their own characteristic scratches nearby. Commonly, two or more scratches are found in the same vicinity, and at times at least a half dozen scratches made at different times can be found in one small area. Wolves also make scratches near their kills or even an old, dry carcass. Like dogs, wolves sometimes wallow on odoriferous objects such as old skunk hides or cow carcasses.

Hunting Methods

> . . . I have many other figures that prove the great loss the wolves cause . . . but it is a well known fact that wolves not only eat meat almost constantly—cattle, horses, or sheep, but they eat the very best obtainable and generally want it fresh. . . .
>
> J. Stokley Ligon, 1916

Wolves hunt at night. Accounts by Bailey (1931), Leopold (1959), and McBride (1980) show that the principal native prey of southwestern wolves was primarily deer, with antelope, mice, and rabbits of less importance. No one knows just how these wolves hunted deer, but they presumably depended on a well developed sense of smell to trail deer and other game to their nighttime beds. When startled in the dark, the deer would be at a disadvantage to the nocturnal wolves, especially on more open, level terrain; here the deer's bounding ability on steep, brushy slopes could not be used to advantage against the wolf's long-winded endurance.

Wolves' hunting techniques changed when ranchers began to settle the West and bring in livestock. Deer, always difficult for canids to obtain, became increasingly scarce under the pressure of subsistence hunting by homesteaders, miners and cowboys. More importantly, livestock were easy picking everywhere. Once set, this table was too good to resist. Unlike mountain lions and some other predators, the adaptable wolves readily abandoned their natural prey and turned almost entirely to cattle. This penchant for livestock is documented in Tables 3.2, 3.3, and 3.4, which show contents of wolf stomachs and scat.

Burros, horses, sheep, and cattle were all prey for wolves. In the case of burros and sheep, adults and young alike were taken, but among horses, colts were usually preferred when available. Cattle, however, provided the great majority of depredations. According to reports on file with the PARC after 1916, the principal victims were large yearling calves, weaned and separated from their mothers. Calves attended by their mothers and other adult animals were taken, but not as readily. If wolves were choosy in their prey selection, it was only to avoid personal injury (McBride 1980).

Considerable evidence from interviews and observations shows that wolf attacks on prey animals were often triggered by the prey animal turning and running, whereas in many instances attacking wolves were

deterred by the belligerent defiance of range bulls or
brood cows with calves. If the cattle did not stampede,
the wolves did not attack. There is no evidence in
southwestern records to indicate that wolves culled
sick, weak, and unfit prey. To the contrary, wolves
were not scavengers; they fed primarily on quality
livestock.

According to McBride (1980), during a cattle stampede the weaker calves or *sanchos* would drop back,
presenting easy targets for wolves. However, the wolves
usually passed them and attacked the better, heavier
animals even though they were harder to kill. When
weaned calves were not available, wolves killed
dependent calves, but not in the numbers or frequency
with which they killed yearlings.

TABLE 3.2

CONTENTS OF 89 WOLF STOMACHS
SENT IN BY PARC HUNTERS, 1918

Contents	Number of Stomachs Containing Item
Beef	13
Horse	2
Sheep and Goat	4
Unclassified meat	2
Deer	1
Acorns	1
Grass, sticks and berries	1
Empty	18
No report	47

Source: Ligon (1918)

TABLE 3.3

ANALYSIS OF 124 WOLF SCATS
FROM MEXICO

Food Item	Number of Scats Containing Item*
Cow	65
Horse and Burro	15
Deer	2
Rodents	1
Unidentified	41

Source: McBride (1980)
*Each scat contained a majority of item listed

TABLE 3.4

STOMACH CONTENTS OF WOLVES
EXAMINED IN MEXICO FROM 1958 TO 1968

Food Item	Number of Stomachs Containing Item
Cow	13
Burro	4
White-tailed Deer	2
Skunk and Cow	1
Horse and Grass	1
Grass	1
Cow and Grass	1
Horse with 1080	1
Empty	10
Unidentifiable	3

Source: McBride (1980)

A cow, freshly killed but not consumed, by wolves. Carcass displays wolves' penchant for attacking from behind and biting rear portions of their victims.

Wolves killed by pursuit and attack from the rear. Livestock kills were made by biting the flank and rump areas; the stomach and bowels were sometimes opened while the victim was running or standing. Yearling calves were generally bitten inside the hind leg and in the rectum; often the tail was sheared off at the body.

On two occasions McBride (1980) found large steers killed from bites under their throats, but the hindquarters of the victims were also damaged and there were lacerations on the nose. Sometimes a pregnant cow ready to give birth was found with the fetus ripped out and partially consumed along with the cow's genitalia. At times, large chunks were bitten from the steer's hindquarters or flanks without killing the animal. Though they remained alive for some time, wounded cattle invariably died. Wolves rarely returned to feed upon them, but instead caught another. Wolves have been known to kill three to four animals in the same night but only feed on one.

Gish (1978) cited several investigators who showed that wolves could fast for long periods, then gorge themselves. Parent wolves would make a kill, often many miles from the den, gorge on the fresh meat, then disgorge it, partially digested, for the young at the den. Others reported that wolves dragged and carried large, heavy portions of cattle carcasses, even swimming them across swift streams, to be deposited at the densite (Young and Goldman 1944).

In the Arizona district annual report for 1925, Musgrave (1925) quoted a letter from Henry C. Boice, manager of the Chiricahua Cattle Company:

> . . . For a number of years the number of wolves running on our range remained about the same. . . . As an indication of how destructive these wolves were, one of our hunters found a den in which young wolves were just old enough to run around. He (the hunter) found 25 calf skulls in and around the den . . . 25 calves that had been killed and dragged in to feed the pups.

Runways

It is well known that individual wolves can cover not only scores, but hundreds, of miles in a few days. Wolves, like other members of the dog family, take care of their feet, traveling trails, roads, washes, and other "easy" routes. These travel circuits, or runways, are favored by individual wolves and by packs investigating or assuming a hunting territory. Traveling together, usually in single file, the animals' pace is a "mile eating trot . . . in which the animals appear to flail their forelegs in a not-graceless fanlike rhythm, managing to look about from side to side as they go" (Gish 1978).

A runway normally runs through open country, over existing roads, trails, or even highways in less populous areas. Runways can vary from a few feet wide to a mile or more, and along the route high vantage points are usually found. The circular shape is often irregular, and its size varies with the abundance or scarcity of game. Scouting courses, which are short detours off the runway, possibly made in search of food, can sometimes be ascertained. Generally, the wolves travel in a counter-clockwise direction on the runway (Young and Goldman 1944).

Descriptions of runways in western Colorado, southern Arizona, and southwestern New Mexico are given by Young and Goldman (1944). Another known wolf runway was through the Mule and Dragoon mountains, north along the east side of the Winchester and Galiuro mountains in Cochise and Graham counties, Arizona, then north to the Aravaipa. The wolf or wolves would then return south through the Galiuros or enter the Pinaleño Mountains, into the foothills of Sulphur Springs Valley. Here much livestock damage was done before concentrated efforts usually removed the offenders.

Since most wolves favored livestock paths or vehicle roads, these were good places to look for sign. When Bayne (1977) noted a wolf had traveled the famous

Double Adobe Creek runway, he knew from past experience that it would be back in a week or two. He estimated that a wolf could make a thirty-five to forty-mile tour in one night.

Sometimes a pair of wolves would travel together on the runways, and traps set close together could catch both animals. If one was caught, the other would often stay nearby and be trapped also (Bayne 1977).

The Cloverdale-Whitewater wolf runway illustrates the appearance of routes traveled by many Mexican wolves entering the United States between 1943 and 1960. Wolves traveling north along the east slope of the Continental Divide would continue north or move west into Barnett Canyon, where they would either drift back into Mexico or move north along the west slope of the Continental Divide in Hidalgo County, New Mexico (Bayne 1977). Those continuing north along the east slope filtered into various creeks and canyons and would end up along Double Adobe Creek near the OK Bar Ranch headquarters. The two runways on the east and west slopes came together north of the Animas Mountains. At this point, the Indian Creek area was used to cross Animas Valley to the Peloncillo Mountains where the wolves could either move into Arizona or return south to Mexico through Guadalupe Canyon or Guadalupe Pass.

SOCIAL ORGANIZATION

Virtually no observations of wolves in the Southwest have been made that were not of persecuted animals under stress. Consequently, no definitive statements

G.A. Nunley, U.S. Fish and Wildlife Service

Historic wolf runway along Indian Creek in Hidalgo County, New Mexico. This was one of several routes that wolves would travel from Mexico to southwest New Mexico and southern Arizona. Such well-known avenues made the border patrol's work easier by concentrating the animals and making trap sets more effective.

can be made about their social behavior, pack organization, or territoriality under normal conditions. Available data suggest that large packs (of six or more wolves) were rare here, which seems reasonable since their natural prey were individual deer. The evolution to large pack behavior would render these conditions a liability rather than an asset. Small-scale social organization appeared to persist even after the advent of large domestic prey; almost all actual accounts were of single animals, pairs, and small packs of family groups or siblings. Social relationships among southwestern wolves were, therefore, relatively simple compared to some of their brethren in the far north and were probably similar to the deer hunting packs described by Kolenosky (1972) in Ontario.

Territoriality and Range

As with social organization, almost nothing is known about the original nature and size of wolf territories in the Southwest. It can only be assumed that the amount of country covered depended on food availability and was somewhat inversely related to the number of wolves present. If so, the introduction of livestock and the arrival of wolf hunters would have disrupted any natural territorial behavior patterns.

Wolves are social animals, and scattered individuals will travel tens and even hundreds of miles in search of a companion. Some wolves captured in the southwestern United States after 1940 must have traveled at least 300 miles from areas in Mexico with breeding populations. Even with the presence of easily taken livestock, individual wolves often operated over a large area before being killed or moving on. These "hunting ranges" were described as thirty-five to seventy-five miles long (McBride 1980); whether these areas can be considered an individual's home range is difficult to state.

Relationship
with
Coyotes

Reports by Rasmussen (1941), Leopold (1959), and others that "where wolves are still plentiful, there are few or no coyotes" cannot be verified—there are simply too few records from areas where wolves were plentiful. Early reports of Ligon (1918), Bailey (1931), and Young and Goldman (1944) do not support this contention. Young and Goldman even state that wolves and coyotes often inhabited the same range. Although they document wolves killing coyotes (and other wolves), there are also numerous references in the literature to coyotes following wolves and subsisting on food they leave behind (Young and Goldman 1944: 250, Gish 1978, McBride 1980). McBride (1980) reported that wolves appeared to totally ignore coyotes, although coyotes took great interest in the wolves' travels. He noted that when a wolf was killing steadily in an area, a swarm of coyotes would be there to take advantage of the wolf's tendency to kill more than it eats.

It may be that the basic habitat preferences of southwest wolves—montane conifer forests, evergreen woodlands and adjacent grassland—were not good coyote habitat when in a pristine state. As ranchers and livestock moved into these areas, the adaptable coyote followed and the combative wolf disappeared, making it difficult to determine whether the two species did, in fact, associate naturally.

REPRODUCTION

Wolves attain sexual maturity at about two years of age—females at one to two years, males sometimes later depending on their social status. Pairing usually first takes place in mid-winter when the animal is about 2½ years old. Once pair bonds are formed, the union is reputed to last for life or until one of the mates dies. McBride (1980) did observe individual adult wolves that made no attempt to travel with other wolves during breeding season, even though few unpaired wolves were available. Although little information is available to support or refute this behavior, the short lifespans of most southwestern wolves make the question of a lifetime pair bond moot. Pair bonds are, however, indisputably strong. Mated pairs show great attachment to each other, seeking out and rejoining their partners after long periods of separation (Young and Goldman 1944, McBride 1980).

The female comes into estrus only once each year. Males, too, only attain breeding condition during this period. Actual mating takes place only during three to five days, and in the Southwest occurs between late December and mid-February. Apparently estrus was about a month earlier for wolves in northern Arizona and New Mexico than in the Sierra Madres. After a gestation period of sixty to sixty-three days, four to eight (extremes are one to eleven) sooty-brown pups are born in the spring—March or April in New Mexico and April to early May in Mexico (Bailey 1931, Young 1944, McBride 1980).

Before the pups, or whelps, are born, the female selects several den sites. These are usually located near an established run in good game country. While the distance to water appears unimportant, a commanding view of the surrounding terrain is favored. One particular site is selected to serve as a birth site and initial nursery. These den sites are described by Bailey (1931), Young (1944), and McBride (1980). If suitable, the same den may be used for many years, provided its occupants are unmolested.

The den is commonly dug out under a rock ledge or at the base of a large tree trunk, usually on a slope and often with some assistance from the male (Young 1944). Dens may be "dug from scratch," or existing holes and cavities may be enlarged. They may have one or several entrances, each often marked by a mound of discarded dirt. The den's main entrance is typically well-hidden, however, often in shrubbery as in an oak or mountain-mahogany thicket.

The entrance is usually so small that the bitch must crawl in on her belly; once inside, the quarters are more spacious but rarely large enough for an adult wolf to stand upright. The distance from the entrance to the bedding chamber where the pups are whelped may be fifty feet. The chamber is of packed earth and unlined.

At birth the pups are blind and helpless, but in five to nine days their eyes open. During the six- to eight-week nursing period the male assists by providing food to the female. He seldom uses the den, only dropping the food at the entrance and remaining on guard during the day from some vantage point. These "lookout stations" are commonly well-marked by the animal's forms in the grass and numerous scats. On the approach of danger, the male will often attempt to lure the intruder away by allowing himself to be seen and howling from a short distance away (Bailey 1931, Young 1944, McBride 1980).

Feces and urine are never voided in the den; the pups' excreta are eaten by the female. Should the den be discovered, or become flea-ridden or dirty, the parents will move the pups to one of the alternate dens. If one of the parents is killed, the mate assumes the parental duties of feeding and moving the pups. After nursing, both sexes hunt for the young, dropping food or disgorging it in piles at the den entrance. If prey is scarce, or the female is without a mate, the wolves may not always make a fresh kill, but instead will clean up previous kills in variance to the usual custom.

The pups first venture out of the den while still nursing, at about three weeks of age. These excursions become longer and more frequent until mid-summer when the pups spend as much time outside the den as inside. Leg bones, scapulars, vertebrae, freshly killed rodents, and even calf skulls are brought to the pups to gnaw and play with. The den's location becomes increasingly evident as the remains of disgorged food, bones, and feces accumulate near the entrance. Wolf dens are vulnerable to discovery at this time, since the parents returning to the pups leave well-marked trails. The wolves may also allow a person to come unusually close before fleeing, and a careful hunter can sometimes get a shot at one of the adults or young.

The pups, now fairly large, may run into the den while others may go with the parents. Both wolf parents are extremely aggressive. If a dog nears the den, they will inevitably attack, resulting in almost certain death for the dog, regardless of size.

By late summer the dens are abandoned, and the 2½- to 3-month-old young follow the parents continually. Although their parents are still feeding them, the pups are being taught to hunt and kill by being taken to the kill sites to finish off mortally wounded animals. If prey is abundant, the number of animals killed increases. This late summer-early fall period proved a vulnerable time for the wolf family. The increase in depredation complaints, the conspicuous presence of several wolves in a small area, and the wolf's strong family ties resulted in the destruction of many family groups by professional wolf hunters.

By October, the young are learning to kill on their own; by December, with the adults preoccupied with amorous matters, they begin making individual forays or remain as a small roving band of litter mates. Contact with the parents is important, however, at this difficult time for these inexperienced youngsters.

Those young that survive usually rejoin their parents and remain with them through the first winter; and some yearlings will even share the same den with the mother and her new litter of pups. Full size is attained between nine and eleven months, and their second winter finds these young animals only loosely associated with their parents, spending most of their time alone or with their siblings. Under natural conditions, many young wolves probably starved when they were forced to new territories or became nonreproducing helpmates to a breeding adult pair. Survivors reached their first breeding season during their third winter, at which time unattached males may have roamed over wide areas looking for a mate. Many stragglers that reached southwestern New Mexico and southeastern Arizona during the 1930 to 1970 period appear to have been males of this age class.

Hybridization

Although instances of wolves breeding with dogs are common in the literature and well-documented among captive animals (see for example, Young and Goldman 1944:180), gray wolves for the most part have maintained their species integrity. McBride (1980), in his extensive experience with wolves in Mexico, neither found nor heard of any instances of wolves hybridizing with dogs until 1980. That year he captured a male wolf that was mated to a ranch dog bitch and from which was sired a litter of pups (C. Carley, personal communication). This is somewhat surprising considering the widespread references to wolf-dog crosses and the availability of ranch dogs in rural Mexico. The tendency for lone males to wander into wolfless areas should have resulted in more incidences of hybrids if cross-breeding in the wild was common. In fact, hybrids are rare in the wild. McBride's observation is supported by Bogan and Mehlhop (1980) who, in examining more than 250 skulls of museum wolves, found only two

specimens that showed any suggestion of other than
wolf parentage. Even these two animals fell well within
the range of measurement for southwestern wolves.
Although museum skulls would be biased toward more
perfect specimens, the fact that these mostly later
collections showed so little evidence of previous hybridization is of interest.

Apparently hybridization in the wild is thwarted by
behavior factors; the wolf's strong pair bond, short
breeding season, and exclusive behavior provided an
effective reproductive barrier. Also, there are no
records of southwestern wolves cross-breeding with
coyotes as reported by Carley (1979) for the red wolf
(*Canis rufus*).

POPULATION
CHARACTERISTICS

The high reproductive potential of the wolf is well
documented in Young (1944), Mech (1970), and elsewhere, but the low densities of wolves reported by
naturalists almost everywhere indicates that this potential was rarely, if ever, realized. Mortality during the
first two years of life must have been high. There is
some reason to believe that under original conditions
natality was influenced by wolf density and food conditions (Vorhies and Mercer, in Gish 1978), but the
factors that controlled southwestern wolf populations
will never be known. The persecuted wolf populations
for which data are available were almost always below
carrying capacity; the biological opportunity to re-
populate their ranks was always present.

Recruitment

McBride (1980) provided figures on embryos from eight females and on litter size from eight dens in Mexico (Table 3.5). These data show a mean litter size of 6.8 before parturition and 4.5 pups in the den, indicating some mortality during or after birth. This loss agrees with the five embryos per pregnant female and four pups per den reported by Vorhies and Mercer (in Gish 1978). These figures for the Mexican wolf are lower than the seven whelps per litter given by Young and Goldman (1944) for wolves in general. The potential recruitment rate was, nonetheless, great even considering the short breeding season and the fact that females do not breed until they are more than two years old, and then probably not each year.

Data from 453 wolves collected by the U.S. Biological Survey and recorded by J. Stokley Ligon when there were still resident wolf populations in New Mexico and Arizona, show about 0.5 pups taken for every adult (Table 3.6). Presumbably pups in dens and weaned pups were both included. Many wolves classified as adults were doubtless nonbreeding animals from 9 to 32 months old; the percentages of the take that were breeding adults, yearlings, and whelps are unknown. If two-thirds of the "adults" were actually nonbreeding yearlings and young two-year-olds, and the sex ratio of 0.86 females per male in Table 3.6 is representative, there would be about three pups per breeding female—a reasonable figure given the reported 4 to 4.5 pups per den. If so, and if the take was representative of the population, we can assume an annual recruitment rate of 30 to 35 percent.

TABLE 3.5

LITTER SIZE OF *CANIS LUPUS BAILEYI*

Den Location	Number of Pups in Litter	Age (months)
Casas Grandes, Chihuahua	5	2
Juan Larga, Chihuahua	8	unborn
Casas Grandes, Chihuahua	7	unborn
Colonia Juarez, Chihuahua	5	3
Santa Clara, Chihuahua	3	1
Santa Clara, Chihuahua	4	unborn
Namiquipa, Chihuahua	3	3
Santiago-Bayacora, Durango	9	unborn
La Flor, Durango	5	2
Los Bahillos de Victor, Durango	8	unborn
Santa Barbara, Durango	5	unborn
Biharro, Durango	6	unborn
Arroyo Hondo, Durango	5	2
Con Duyenos de Nayar, Durango	6	3
San Pedro, Durango	4	1
Tierras Prietas, Sonora	7	unborn
Average litter size	5.63	

Source: McBride (1980)

Sex Ratios

It is interesting to contrast Ligon's sex ratio data (Table 3.6) with Arnold Bayne's collections between 1944 and 1966 (Table 2.1). Ligon's data, collected from resident wolves in Arizona and New Mexico, are the earliest and largest samples from the Southwest.

TABLE 3.6

WOLF AGE AND SEX RATIO DATA
COLLECTED BY J. STOKLEY LIGON,
1916 TO 1921

Year	No. of Wolves Taken	Males	Females	(Female: Male Ratio)	Adults	Pups	(Young: Adult Ratio)
1916	69	—	—	—	33	36	(1.1)
1917	85	34	34	(1.00)	68	17	(0.3)
1918	111	40	41	(1.00)	81	30	(0.4)
1919	65	32	20	(0.63)	52	13	(0.3)
1920	67	—	—	—	46	21	(0.5)
1921	56	27	20	(0.74)	33	23	(0.7)
Total	453	133	115	(0.86)	313	140	(0.5)

Source: Ligon (1916 to 1921)

These data show relatively narrow sex ratios (0.86 females per male), particularly in the earlier years. After 1918, the sex ratios appeared to diverge further from a 1:1 ratio, with males becoming more prevalent in the take as resident wolf populations decreased. Bayne's data, collected from a decimated population and consisting of 34 stragglers, show a sex ratio of only 0.48 females per male. These data are explained by the tendency of males to wander farther north and to break new territory or reoccupy old territory (C. Carley, personal communication). This explanation is supported by a sample of 16 females and 12 males (1.3 females per male) taken by McBride (1980) from still extant populations in the Sierra Madres.

Sex ratio data from the American Museum of Natural History (Nunley 1977) and from Bogan and Mehlhop (1980), based on several collections of south-western wolves, show sex ratios imbalanced toward males: 0.7 females per male (N = 34) and 0.62 females per male (N = 168). Many of these museum specimens are from the same areas and time as Bayne's were and are subject to the same collecting biases; there was probably also a tendency to supply collections with larger males when a number of specimens were avail-able, and males may be more trap prone than females because of behavior differences.

Disparate sex ratios favoring males were also found in wolf populations in Minnesota, and Mech (1975) concluded that this might be a function of more male pups being produced when competition for food was intense. Knowlton (1972) and Andrews and Boggess (1978) also found a predominance of males in most coyote samples. Verme (1969) found that white-tailed deer does produced a significantly greater number of male fawns when experimentally fed on restricted diets. More recently, Verme and Ozoga (1981) reported that the disproportionate number of male white-tailed deer produced might be a result of disrupted or delayed breeding. Such a phenomenon could also explain the increase in the proportion of male wolves in later collections.

Mortality

Although wolves have been reported to suffer from mange (Gish 1978), as well as being susceptible to rabies and plague, the major causes of natural mortality in the pre-settlement Southwest were probably related to the difficulty of obtaining game and the ravages of age. When game was scarce, intraspecific rivalry, always a regulating mechanism, must have become intense strife. Those animals unable to hold a territory were hard pressed to kill enough game in marginal areas to maintain hunting prowess and attain breeding condition. The advent of a steady and assured food supply in the form of livestock may have boosted wolf population levels, but these gains were offset by increased mortality at the hands of ranchmen. Almost all documented wolf mortality since World War I has been related to predator control efforts.

There was not a stockman on the Currumpaw who would not readily have given the value of many steers for the scalp of any one of Lobo's band, but they seemed to possess charmed lives, and defied all manner of devices to kill them.

Ernest Thompson Seton, 1898

4

Old One Toe
And Other
Famous Wolves

IT WAS COMMON PRACTICE during the heyday of wolf trapping for hunters to create "campfire legends" about certain wolves. Individualizing wolves was appealing because it personalized the trapper's efforts against his adversary. The greater the animal's cunning, or the larger its toll among livestock, the greater the glory and service of its captor. As with most rumors, when retold often enough they grew out of proportion.

As wolves became scarce, every wolf encountered by PARC hunters was considered an individual, differing in some way from the others. Many were crippled, lacking toes, a foot, or even a leg. Some were reported to lurk around ranch houses and be of distinctive color.

Young (1944) listed a number of "famous" wolves, including in the Southwest the Currumpaw Wolf of New Mexico, popularized by Ernest Thompson Seton (1929), Arizona's Spring Valley Wolf, and Old Aguila.

155

Soon after he took office as Arizona district supervisor of the PARC, Musgrave (1921) publicized the Spring Valley Wolf: "Early in September [1920], Mr. Fred Willis was detailed to the same range [between Williams and the Grand Canyon] and . . . got one of the most *famous* wolves in the State." The Spring Valley Wolf was actually two wolves that ranged for four or five years, sometimes together although more often separately, from the Grand Canyon to Kendrick Mountain. The darker, younger wolf was killed by a rancher named Saunderson. The second Spring Valley wolf, older and almost white, was poisoned by PARC agent Willis while he was after coyotes. One of several characteristics of the Spring Valley wolves, in addition to killing stock valued at $2,000 to $2,500 a year, was their habit of ". . . visiting back yards and playing with ranch dogs" (Musgrave 1921, Gish 1978).

Gish (1978) quotes Everett Mercer's tale of another wolf farther south in Santa Cruz County, Arizona:

> There was one lobo down along the border near Ruby, that would invariably rip out the flank of a big calf, steer or yearling. Just enough that the bowels came out. He always attacked the same way from the rear and flank, feeding, just a few bites of flank at a time, while following the cripple for a day or so until it died. Then it would cut out another fat calf and repeat the performance. It never varied.

PARC hunter Bill Casto finally snagged this wolf, but it escaped, leaving two toes in the trap; Old One Toe always left his distinguishing mark after that, like the single scratch of a ten penny nail, literally pointing directly at each trap set for him.

Gish (1978) went on to relate how Phil Clark, a Santa Cruz County rancher, found this peculiar, single-toe scratch mark and notified PARC trapper, Johnny Ehn. Ehn searched and found Old One Toe's distinctive signature on top of some cattle tracks in the dust.

Mercer visited the area after Phil Clark's telephone call and noticed some sets that Ehn had not reported. He suspected that Ehn, on government salary, was trying to bootleg the catch for private bounty. Ehn admitted that he had intended to bootleg the wolf, but had not been able to catch him.

It took Johnny Ehn several more years to catch Old One Toe after it had gone in and out of Mexico uncounted times. Always, Ehn found the characteristic single-toe scratch mark at his sets. As always, the trick was to know the range and get out ahead of the wolf, but not many Mexican wolves were as astute as One Toe.

In 1916, Musgrave made record of the notorious Chiricahua Wolf:

> One of the most wiley and destructive wolves in this state was taken by A. W. Mills in the Chiricahua Mountains in June. This wolf was known to have run the full length of the Chiricahuas for the past four years, and though other packs of wolves have drifted through from Mexico, this wolf has never joined with them for any length of time, but has played the Lone Wolf game, killing a yearling about every four days, and never returning to the carcass.

Old Aguila (Musgrave 1924) deserves a word as the most famous Arizona wolf. Taken by Charlie Gillham, later a prolific outdoor writer, Old Aguila had an excellent press agent.

Her statistics were impressive: ranging in western Maricopa County at Sonoran Desert and semidesert elevations far lower than usual for a wolf, she was credited with killing many thousands of dollars worth of cattle and sheep from 1916 to 1924. One night she reportedly killed sixty-five sheep, and forty another night. According to Gish (1978), "it had a retinue like the tail of a comet, consisting of a large satellite band of coyotes that got fat on 'Old Aguila's' leavings."

Like a number of famous wolves, Old Aguila was whitish in color. Eluding hundreds of gunners and amateur and professional trappers for eight years, when finally killed she brought one of the largest bounties ever offered in Arizona—$500.

In his 1925 annual report, Musgrave stated that:

> . . . the catching of a wolf is not so much a difficult matter as the locating of his range. We have found during the past two years since wolves have gotten down to a very few individuals, that they travel long distances, and change their ranges, possibly hunting for other wolves, possibly fearing the consequences of what happened to the remainder of the kind. At any rate, they are more restless than when they ran in packs, and are not so regular in their habits.

Unfortunately, for posterity if not for science, as wolves became scarce the campfire legends also became history, and the tale bearers turned to other things.

There was an occasional exception. On April 3, 1952 Mercer reported that a PARC hunter trapped a lone wolf on Charles Prude's Ranch in the Galiuro Range in Graham County, Arizona. Prude told the

PARC hunter that this wolf had been ranging in the area since December. A number of local ranchers judged from the wolf's manner that it might have been in captivity at one time. Its tracks were seen frequently around the Prude barn and other outbuildings, and Mrs. Prude saw the wolf through a window one evening. The wolf had also been seen at various times by Prude and several of the ranch helpers and by a lion hunter working in the vicinity. Another distinction of the Prude wolf was that it was heard howling a number of times, once in full daylight.

The Prude wolf was reported to have been shot and wounded by a motorist and was recovering from what appeared to be a gunshot wound when he was trapped (Gish 1978).

Las Margaritas was the name McBride gave to a wolf that operated over a large territory from the Zacatecas-Durango border through almost the entire state of Durango. McBride (1980) described an episode that began during the late 1960s when this wolf started killing yearling steers and heifers at Las Margaritas Ranch. The wolf was missing two toes from its left front foot, and its experience with traps left a memory that served it well; all efforts to poison or trap this wolf were futile. In spring 1970, Las Margaritas moved north to the Mazatlán-Durango Highway and began killing steers on the El Carmen and Santa Barbara ranches on the west side of the railroad between Durango and Regocijo. McBride, trapping in Durango for the Cattlemen's Union, had heard about this wolf when he was trying to catch a pair of yearling wolves. By March he had taken the yearling female, and the male had gone. Las Margaritas then came to McBride.

Las Margaritas.

In April depredations started again; McBride at first thought the young male had returned; but when he saw the track in a dusty trail, he noticed the missing toes—trademark of Las Margaritas. After reportedly killing thirteen steers, the wolf went west in May and, after killing more cattle, disappeared. In June Las Margaritas returned to Rancho Santa Barbara where it killed eighteen steers. Characteristically, the wolf seldom used the same trail twice. If it came into a pasture by a log road, it left by a cow trail.

McBride was certain he could catch the wolf if he could get it near a trap. Finally, at the end of July, the wolf came down a washed-out log road and passed one of McBride's trap sets. The wolf smelled the trap, turned back, and trotted up to it, barely missing the trigger with the gap caused by the missing toes. The wolf then apparently suspected the trap and left the road. It did not return until September; ninety-six steers and yearling heifers were reported killed in the next eight months on one ranch alone.

In October McBride found where Las Margaritas had urinated on a small juniper beside a logging road; he carefully placed a set there. Two weeks later the wolf passed by the trap, advanced a few steps towards it, and then ran down the road. The only scent on the bush was its own, and McBride could not understand how the wolf knew the trap was there. Las Margaritas then moved to a new area where it resumed killing.

A pair of wolves showed up in this area in November and began killing in the same pasture in which Las Margaritas was operating. Several days after their arrival, McBride picked up fresh tracks that the two

wolves had made before the dew. He also saw Las
Margaritas's tracks but they were made after the dew
had formed. While trailing them, McBride noted that
whenever the male of the pair left the road to make a
scent station, Las Margaritas never investigated but
continued down the road. Finally, the pair of wolves
came to one of McBride's traps, and the female was
caught. When Las Margaritas came to where the trap
had been pulled out of the ground, the wolf left the road
and disappeared until December.

In late December reports of Las Margaritas killings
began anew, but in a different pasture. Traps were set
daily on all the wolf's travel routes, but again the wolf
seldom returned to a previously used trail. In January
McBride made three blind sets in a narrow cow trail in
the gap of a mountain, convinced that the wolf would
not go to any baited site. Two weeks passed before Las
Margaritas came down the mountain divide and hit the
cow trail about a hundred yards above the traps. About
fifteen feet from the first trap, she left the trail and went
around the set. Large evergreen oaks were on either
side of the trail, and windblown leaves hid the traps.
McBride had stepped from his horse to a steer hide
while setting the traps, the dirt had been removed by a
sifter, and the traps had been boiled in oak leaves. The
trap could not have been better concealed. Nonetheless,
the wolf returned to the trail without being caught and
approached the second set on the other side of a pine
tree that had fallen across the trail. Again the wolf left
the trail and went around the trap. As it neared the third
trap, the wolf left the trail before getting to the trap site.
On trailing up the trap, McBride later found a coyote in
it. The wolf had left, and for about a week nothing was

heard of Las Margaritas until it began killing about fifteen miles to the west. By March, McBride was convinced that he would never catch this wolf.

At times, McBride noticed that Las Margaritas had investigated a campfire along the road where log truck drivers would stop and cook. He decided to set a trap near a road that the wolf was sure to come down if it continued to kill in this pasture. He built a fire over the trap and let it burn out. At the edge of the ashes he placed a piece of dried skunk hide.

On March 15 the wolf came down the road, winded the ashes and skunk hide, and walked over to investigate. Las Margaritas was caught by the crippled foot and the trap held. There was much celebration among the ranchers the following day. In eleven months of intensive effort and several thousand miles on horseback, McBride had managed to get the wolf near a trap only four times.

Another infamous wolf, claimed to be the last one in Texas, eluded the efforts of Montie Wallace, one-time foreman of the Downie Ranch in southern Pecos County, Texas, who did considerable trapping on a contract basis during the early 1900s. Tanned wolfskins were used as throw rugs on the floor and as covers on tables, but the skin of one wolf, the great white lobo, held a special place in the Wallace home, usually hanging on the living room wall. In July 1972, a year before he died, Wallace described in a taped interview with Clayton Williams, Sr. (1974) how he killed The White Lobo:

> The last lobo in T. M. Pyle country was a white one. I
> had heard of it for five years. A. M. Cone said he
> would pay five hundred dollars to anybody who would

kill the white lobo. That was a lot of money in those days. I trapped and trapped. I could never understand why I had not succeeded in catching the white wolf.

One day I was on my way to T. M. Pyle country. Because it had rained, I figured it would be easier to travel on the Round Mountain rather than the Sanderson road. I had just passed the Round Mountain hill when the white lobo crossed the road just twenty-five steps ahead of me. I traveled at least twenty-five steps before it saw me. I figured then that it couldn't hear or it would have heard me as I traveled noisily along. It then was startled and ran fifty yards and stopped and looked back. I was almost certain that there were more wolves in that vicinity, but I didn't have my gun and I couldn't do anything about it. I was almost certain that the wolf couldn't hear or it would not have let me get that close to it when my horse was jogging along the road. That was the year before I finally killed it. In 1925, I went back to the T. M. Pyle country working for Downie, who sent me word that there was a lobo in the Pyle country. Ed Downie had a doctor visiting him from San Antonio who wanted to go deer hunting. One morning the doctor wanted to go with me on the wolf hunt and I agreed to take him. I knew the wolf was killing and staying in the Clarot country. If I could frighten it out of hiding I might be able to kill it. We rode to Clarot Hill in the Pyle pasture in the tall hills. Halfway up Clarot Hill we came to where two canyons joined in the mountain. These canyons opened up onto a main canyon that ran down to the ranch.

The wolves had hidden in the draw where the two canyons ran into the large canyon. I looked in there and couldn't see anything. In our search, we rode down right in the middle of the draw and then to the top of the canyon. Suddenly, the white lobo got up within thirty feet of where we had passed by. We had passed close by and on three sides of the wolf without it being aware of us. To me this indicated that it was both deaf and had no sense of smell or it would have scented us. It ran into the draw where there was a lot of brush. I only got a glimpse of it every once in awhile. Even so, I took two shots at it and missed.

I told the doctor to stay on the top and I rode across the canyon which was about three quarter of a mile distance. When I got on the hill I saw it trotting along on a cow trail. I then got off my horse, took my gun and shot at her. She just stopped. I shot again and she fell over backward. The first shot killed her. The second one knocked her down. Both shots hit her in the heart just an inch away from each other. She was a fairly old female, all snow white, except a gray-tipped tail. Her tail was stiff as a board. She couldn't hear or smell, that's why I hadn't been able to catch her with scented and baited traps (Scudday 1977).

5

A Dire Prognosis

BY 1970 THE GRAY WOLF, OR LOBO as it is better known in the Southwest, had been extirpated over most of its former range in the United States and Mexico. In 1982 no wolves or sign of wolves were reported in Mexico. Through financing by ranchers in the form of bounties and hired trappers, and salaried professional wolf hunters provided by the U.S. government, resident wolves had been effectively removed from the southwest United States. The Intermountain, Plains, and Mogollon races were extinct. Only the Mexican wolf remained in the Sierra Madre Occidental in Mexico, where the limits of its rapidly shrinking range were largely undetermined.

In 1977 the U.S. Fish and Wildlife Service's Office of Endangered Species, in cooperation with the Mexican government, commissioned Roy T. McBride, then working as a professional hunter in Mexico, to document the remaining distribution of wolves and to estimate population numbers. This survey was conducted in the winter and spring of 1977. Limited time and money made it impossible for McBride to examine the entire historic range of the wolf in Mexico. Instead, he investigated those areas where wolves were known to be present in recent years.

To survey wolf numbers, it was first necessary to locate areas where wolves were still thought to exist. Knowing that wolves are closely associated with cattle, McBride employed some unusual means to locate wolf populations. For example, banks make livestock loans in Mexico just as they do in the United States, and livestock are usually put up as collateral. On trips to inspect cattle secured by these loans, bank examiners hear many excuses for cattle shortages, including wolf predation. In one instance, McBride interviewed a young man seeking a loan in a bank in Durango, who told of only one place where wolves were known to be present; McBride believed this report was accurate because he was then working that area and knew wolves were there.

Another excellent information source was the cattle buyers who travel into remote areas, often purchasing cattle from Indians who live deep in the Sierra. These small-time cowmen, familiar with extensive areas of backcountry, hear of wolf and lion depredations. The cattlemen's association of each state also provided reports of wolf problems. Every source of information was sought, and reliable leads were checked by McBride personally.

Only widely scattered, small populations of wolves were found, with occasional stragglers occurring in other parts of the wolf's formerly extensive range. By spring 1977, McBride had located at least twelve wolves in the state of Durango and six in the state of Chihuahua. As confirmation, he took seven wolves from these areas during the autumn of 1977 and in early 1978. Table 5.1 documents these catches as well as others taken by co-workers and ranchers under his direction.

These wolves were found in a variety of habitats, but since ungulates are their principal prey, most lived in the montane forests and oak country possessing better browse and grass. These remaining wolf habitats are at elevations above 4,500 feet, where greater rainfall promotes better grazing.

Because only scattered remnants of wolf packs remain, McBride found it impossible to determine if territories constitute home ranges (McBride 1980). Wolves wander over huge areas, and cattle, their alternate prey, are plentiful wherever they roam; at times wolves are driven long distances from their normal mountain habitats. Mining, logging, firewood cutting, goat herding, and constant deer hunting continually disrupt wolf activity patterns. Consequently, they wander large areas, change routes constantly, and sometimes fail to return to areas they once used frequently.

The largest breeding population McBride found was a widely scattered group of approximately fifteen animals in a large area southwest of Durango, Durango (Map B, page 11). Much of this country is inaccessible by vehicle, and some is Indian territory. Logging activity in the accessible portions causes the wolves to move constantly. Trapping is slow and difficult in this rugged mountain region; at times, little or no wolf sign is found, only to reappear months later.

TABLE 5.1

CONFIRMED RECORDS OF WOLVES TAKEN FROM 1972 TO 1978 IN CHIHUAHUA AND DURANGO, MEXICO

Location	Date	Physical Evidence	Total number of wolves
S of Casas Grandes, Chih.	1973	trapped	1
Santa Clara Valley, Chih.	1976	trapped	2
Santa Clara Valley, Chih.	1976	shot	1
Santa Clara Valley, Chih.	1976	poisoned	1
Santa Clara Valley, Chih.	1977-78	tracks	5
Sierra de las Tunas, Chih.	1977	trapped	3
Sierra del Nido, Chih.	1978	live trapped*	2
Near Regocijo, Dgo.	1973	trapped	7
Near La Flor, Dgo.	1972	trapped	2
Near La Flor, Dgo.	1972	shot	4
Near La Flor, Dgo.	1977	shot	1
Near Penoles, Dgo.	1977	shot	2
Near Penoles, Dgo.	1977	trapped	1
Near La Flor, Dgo.	1977	tracks	5
Near Cebollas, Dgo.	1978	tracks	2
Near Arroyo Hondo, Dgo.	1977	tracks	1
Near Guacamaya, Dgo.	1977	tracks	2
Near Coneto, Dgo.	1978	live trapped*	4
Near San Jose, Dgo.	1977	shot	2
Near Viscaino, Dgo.	1977	poisoned	1
Near Viscaino, Dgo.	1977	shot	1
Near Las Isgalias, Dgo.	1978	poisoned	3

Source: McBride (1980)
*Indicates wolves trapped for captive breeding program in United States.

A second area harboring a small breeding population of wolves was north and west of Durango and
east of Tepehuanes, Durango. This area is also only
partially accessible. These animals are difficult to
reach although a high human population inhabits the
region, with active mining and logging industries.
McBride estimated that six wolves inhabited this area.

A third area containing wolves was north of Chihuahua, Chihuahua, and east of Casas Grandes, Chihuahua
(Map B). This was a breeding population, but as of
1977 McBride knew of only two adult wolves there.
The area's accessibility by vehicle and horseback has
led to the animals' exposure to traps and poison.

A fourth area that may harbor wolves and had wolves
in 1977 is the Sierra del Nido in Chihuahua, including
the mountains to the south surrounding Santa Clara
Valley. McBride estimated this population at probably
less than six wolves.

Other areas from which reliable reports were received
(Map B) were not checked, but assuming their similarity
to those investigated, McBride thought it probable that
some fifty wolves remain in Mexico. Although their
reproductive potential is high, the actual number of
wolves can fluctuate greatly depending on denning
success, or conversely, the success of the ranchers'
predator control efforts. None of the wolves is immune
to persecution.

Roy McBride told Dan Gish that in 1981 he had had
no reports of wolves in Mexico and had found no sign
on his hunts. Although this does not mean that the wolf
is completely gone from its final southwest strongholds
in Durango and Chihuahua, it is indicative of its plight.

As was often the case in the past, any obituary would probably be premature, but by no means uncertain. The wolf is certainly doomed to extinction as a member of the southwest's fauna, if, in fact, any occur. As McBride has noted, they cannot be saved.

How can this be? Wolves still live in such long-populated countries as Spain, Greece, Yugoslavia, and Italy (Mech 1970). Certainly, then, there must be room for a small number of wolves in the rugged Southwest, with its large national parks, forests, and wilderness areas. Cannot we, who find our challenges in the frontier outdoors, afford a few wolves as do the Greeks and Italians? I think not.

The difference between those countries where wolves still occur and the Southwest is that the wolf was never completely eliminated from southern Europe. If wolves had somehow managed to persist in and around Grand Canyon National Park, for example, or in what is now Guadalupe Mountains National Park, or in the Blue Range and Gila wilderness areas, the outlook for them in the Southwest would not be so dire. They would be troublesome but valued assets of the national park and national forest system. The fact is, though, that wolves did not survive anywhere in the southwest United States, and any token population would now have to be reintroduced.

The difference between protection and introduction is great. To reintroduce wolves would require enormous administrative commitment and public support—two conditions that do not occur now or in the foreseeable future. The legal ramifications alone are enough to dissuade even the most ardent supporter of a natural biological system—not to mention administrators with political responsibilities. A resident pack would not confine itself to any administrative area. Those responsible for a reintroduction effort could find themselves liable for any losses incurred from the animals' release.

Any reintroduction would have to be accompanied by controversial contingency programs and control policies coordinated with game and fish departments and their commissions. Ranchers and their organizations would have to be mollified—no easy task—and hunters and trappers accommodated. In addition, state and local government support would have to be obtained. In essence, almost all would have to support such a program; almost no one could oppose it.

It took a dedicated and conscientious effort on the part of the federal government and state cooperators to eliminate the wolf from the West for the benefit of the stockmen. It is, therefore, ironic that the belated task of preserving the Mexican wolf went to the agency that had insured the wolf's destruction beyond the point of no return. To date it has been easier to control "noxious" species than to recover "endangered" ones. Now that the U.S. Fish and Wildlife Service is actively involved in the recovery of threatened species, it is unfortunate that the wolf is no longer extant in the U.S. half of the Southwest.

Certainly some later administrators can be faulted for not having a more enlightened attitude. No real justification can be given for continuing to take wolves into the 1940s, 1950s, and even the 1960s—especially in places such as Fort Huachuca, some Indian reservations, and in Mexico. It should have been apparent that the wolf had been reduced to a manageable menace. There was no *need* to get the last wolf any more than it was necessary to take the last wolves from Grand Canyon National Park and Game Preserve during the deer irruption in the 1920s.

According to Gish, a number of people, beginning with the late Chuck Hanson, curator of the Arizona-Sonora Desert Museum, advocated a captive breeding program so that the Mexican wolf would not be entirely lost as were the other three southwest races. Some expressed hope that such a program would provide stock for an eventual transplant to a select wilderness. This is all fine, but such prospects appear nil.

It must be stated that the Mexican Wolf Recovery Team has accepted that challenge. This group of dedicated professional men and women are committed to developing the means to reintroduce a wolf population to specific areas where they would become part of a managed ecosystem. They have secured a captive stock of pure Mexican wolves and developed a recovery plan for the eventual success of such a venture. Their efforts are worthy of support.

One nagging question remains, although admittedly of an academic nature. Why were the efforts of the PARC, and state and private cooperators, successful against the wolf but not the mountain lion? The lion was persecuted just as heavily, yet it has maintained itself throughout most of its southwestern range while the wolf was eliminated. Unlike the bear, which had sportsmen allies (even the grizzly received some protection, although too little, too late), wolves and lions held the animosity of ranchers and sportsmen (see for example O'Conner 1939). The reasons are both social and biological.

Wolf hunters were the most appreciated of the predator control agents. Because the PARC hunters and their supervisors wanted to be of value to the biological survey, more emphasis was always placed on taking wolves over other predators. This attitude made it politically feasible to permanently field specialized wolf hunters at government expense. Regardless of the number of wolf incursions, these men were always there, always available and always giving the wolf top priority. The wolf was the victim of preventive maintenance.

The lions' preference for venison and heavy, brushy cover was an advantage, especially in areas where deer were abundant. Cattle are not as readily taken by lions, and when they are, they are not as conspicuous as wolf kills (McBride 1977). Because wolves were almost always stock killers, they were sure to draw the wrath of the stockmen; the lion was sometimes ignored.

Both wolves and lions have high potential reproductive rates and can cope with high losses. Both cover wide areas, and when not tied down with family chores, are constantly on the move. The wolf, however, forms strong pair bonds and, unlike the lion, both mates raise the young. Strong family ties, a prolonged weaning period, and a tendency toward sociability worked against the wolf. Their howls announced their presence and made them conspicuous. These traits made them easier to locate and kill. Also, once located, the wolf was susceptible to traps *and* poison. Lions take time to trap and are rarely poisoned. Their control usually requires a skilled hunter with trained dogs.

In the end, I suspect it was a combination of the persistence of its persecutors and the susceptibility of remnant family groups to poison that brought about the wolf's downfall. Although most wolves were reported taken in traps, the use of poison was probably an important factor in their final destruction. The wolf's use of discernible runways not only made for easy trap setting, it also allowed the concentration of innumerable poison stations. These stations, especially when baited with Compound 1080, could be devastating to younger animals. More than fifty years of constant effort finally destroyed the wolf. That it took that long is a fitting testimonial to his tenacity.

MARILYN HOFF STEWART

Bibliography

ALLEN, J.A. 1895. On a collection of mammals from Arizona and New Mexico made by Mr. W.W. Price, with field notes by the collector. *Bull. Amer. Mus. Nat. Hist.* 7(6):193–258.

ANDERSON, S. 1972. Mammals of Chihuahua. *Bull. Amer. Mus. Nat. Hist.* 148:151–410.

ANDERSON, T.E. 1969. Identifying, evaluating, and controlling wildlife damage. pp. 497–520 *in* R.H. Giles edition of *Wildlife Mgmt. Techniques.* The Wildlife Society, 622 pp.

ANDREWS, R.D. and E.K. BOGGESS. 1978. Ecology of coyotes in Iowa. pp. 249–265 *in* Bekoff, M. *Coyotes—biology, behavior and management.* Academic Press, N.Y.

ARMSTRONG, D. 1972. Distribution of mammals in Colorado. *Monog. Mus. Nat. Hist.,* Univ. of Kansas 3:1–415.

ATZERT, S.P. 1971. A review of sodium monofluoroacetate (compound 1080) its properties, toxicology and use in predator and rodent control. *U.S.D.I. Fish and Wildlife Service Spec. Sci. Rept.* 146.

177

BAHRE, C.J. 1977. Land use history of the Research Ranch, Elgin, Arizona. *J. Ariz. Acad. Sci.* Vol. 12, Suppl. 2:1–32.

BAILEY, V. 1905. Biological survey of Texas, *U.S.D.A. Bur. Biol. Surv. N. Amer. Fauna* 25:1–222.

———. 1907. Wolves in relation to stock, game and the National Forest Reserves. *U.S.D.A. Forest Service Bull.* 72:1–31.

———. 1908. Destruction of wolves and coyotes— results obtained during 1907. *U.S.D.A. Bur. Biol. Surv. Circ.* 63:1–11.

———. 1909. Key to animals on which wolf and coyote bounties are often paid. *U.S.D.A. Bur. Biol. Surv.* 69:1–3.

———. 1931. Mammals of New Mexico. *U.S.D.A. Bur. Biol. Surv. N. Amer. Fauna* 53:1–412.

BAIRD, S.F. 1859. *United States and Mexican boundary survey: part II—Zoology of the boundary.* Mammals, pp. 1–62. U.S.D.I., Washington, D.C.

BAKER, R.H. 1956. Mammals of Coahuila, Mexico. *Univ. Kansas Publ., Mus. Nat. Hist.* 9:125–335.

BAKER, R.H. and B. VILLA R. 1960. Distribucion geographica y poblacion actuales del lobo gris en Mexico. *Anal. Inst. Biol. Univ. Nacional Mexico* 30:369–374.

BAKER, R.H. and J.K. GREER. 1962. Mammals of the Mexican state of Durango. *Publ. Mus. Michigan St. Univ., Biol. Ser.* 2:25–154.

BARTLETT, J.R. 1854. *Personal narrative of explorations and incidents.* 2 vols. New York. 1125 pp.

BAYNE, A.R. 1977. Personal communication to G.L. Nunley. *In* Nunley, G.L. 1977. *The Mexican gray wolf in New Mexico.* U.S. Fish and Wildl. Serv. Rep. Albuquerque. 80 pp.

BLISS, C.F. 1921–1922. Predatory animal control. New Mexico District. *Annual Repts.* U.S.D.A. Bur. Biol. Survey.

BOGAN, M.A. and P. MEHLHOP. 1980. Systematic relationships of gray wolves (*Canis lupus*) in southwestern North America. National Mus. of Natural History Report to the New Mexico Dept. of Game and Fish. *Endangered Species F.A. Report E*:1–237.

BROWN, D.E. and R.J. GUTIERREZ. 1980. Sex ratios, sexual selection, and sexual dimorphism in quails. *J. Wild. Manage.* 44:198–202.

BROWN, D.E. and C.H. LOWE. 1980. Biotic communities of the Southwest (Map). *U.S.D.A. Forest Service, Rocky Mtn. Forest and Range Exper. Stat. Gen. Tech. Report* RM-78.

BURKHOLDER, B.L. 1959. Movements and behavior of a wolf pack in Alaska. *J. Wild. Manage.* 23(1):1–11.

BURT, W. 1938. Faunal relationships and geographic distribution of mammals in Sonora, Mexico. *Misc. Publ. Mus. Zool., Univ. Michigan* 39:1–77.

CAIRE, W. 1978. The distribution and zoogeography of the mammals of Sonora, Mexico. Unpubl. PhD. dissert., Univ. New Mexico, Albuquerque. 613 pp.

CARLEY, C.J. 1979. Status summary: the red wolf (*Canis rufus*). U.S. Fish and Wildl. Serv., Albuquerque. *Endangered Species Rep.* 7:1–36.

CATES, C.E. 1939–1941. Predatory animal control. New Mexico District. *Annual Repts.* U.S.D.A. Bur. Biol. Survey.

COCKRUM, E.L. 1960. *The recent mammals of Arizona.* Univ. of Arizona Press, Tucson. 276 pp.

CONNER, D.E. 1956. *Joseph Reddeford Walker and the Arizona adventure.* Univ. of Oklahoma Press, Norman. 364 pp.

COUES, E. 1867. Notes on a collection of mammals from Arizona. *Proc. Acad. Sci. of Philadelphia.* 19:133–136.

DALQUEST, W.W. 1953. Mammals of the Mexican state of San Luis Potosi. *Louisiana St. Univ. Studies, Biol. Sci. Ser.* 1:1–229.

180   Bibliography

DAVIS, G.P., JR. 1973. Man and wildlife in Arizona: the presettlement era, 1823–1864. M.S. Thesis. Dept. of Biol. Sci., Univ. of Arizona, Tucson. 251 pp.

DAY, A.M. 1949. Statement of policy for use of Compound 1080 (sodium monofluoroacetate). U.S.D.I. Fish and Wildl. Serv. Washington, D.C.

DICE, L.R. 1943. *The biotic provinces of North America.* Univ. of Mich. Press, Ann Arbor. 78 pp.

ECHOLS, W.C. 1927. Predatory animal control. New Mexico District. *Feb.–May, Oct.–Dec. Narratives.* U.S.D.A. Bur. Biol. Surv.

_____. 1928. Predatory animal control. New Mexico District. *Jan. Narrative.* U.S.D.A. Bur. Biol. Surv.

EMORY, W.H. 1848. *Notes of a military reconnaissance.* Washington, D.C. 613 pp.

FINDLEY, J.S., A.H. HARRIS, D.E. WILSON, and C. JONES. 1975. *Mammals of New Mexico.* Univ. of New Mexico Press, Albuquerque. 360 pp.

FLADER, S.L. 1974. *Thinking like a mountain—Aldo Leopold and the evolution of an ecological attitude toward deer, wolves, and forests.* Univ. of Missouri Press, Columbia. 284 pp.

FOSTER, B.E. 1931–1937. Predatory animal control. Arizona District. *Annual Repts.* U.S.D.A. Bur. Biol. Surv., U.S.D.I. Fish and Wildl. Serv.

GATLIN, J.C. 1930–1938. Predatory animal control. New Mexico District. *Annual Repts.* U.S.D.A. Bur. Biol. Surv., U.S.D.I. Fish and Wildl. Serv.

_____. 1930a. Predatory animal control. New Mexico District. Quarter ending Dec. 31. *Narrative.* U.S.D.A. Bur. Biol. Surv.

_____. 1931a. Predatory animal control. New Mexico District. Quarter ending Mar. 31. *Narrative.* U.S.D.A. Bur. Biol. Surv.

_____. 1931b. Predatory animal control. New Mexico District. Quarter ending Dec. 31. *Narrative.* U.S.D.A. Bur. Biol. Surv.

GILCHRIST, D.A. 1930. Predatory animal control. Arizona District. *Annual Rept.* U.S.D.A. Bur. Biol. Surv.

GISH, D.M. 1978. An historical look at the Mexican gray wolf (*Canis lupus baileyi*) in early Arizona Territory and since statehood. U.S.D.I. Fish and Wildl. Serv. Rept. 204 pp.

GOLDMAN, E.A. 1937. The wolves of North America. *J. Mamm.* 18:37–45.

_____. 1944. Classification of wolves. Part 2 *in* Young, S.P. and E.A. Goldman. *The wolves of North America.* Amer. Wildl. Inst., Washington, D.C. pp. 389–636.

GOLDMAN, E.A. and R.T. MOORE. 1945. The biotic provinces of Mexico. *J. Mamm.* 26:347–360.

GRAY, A.E. 1926. Predatory animal control. New Mexico District. *Dec. Narrative.* U.S.D.A. Bur. Biol. Surv.

_____. 1927–1929. Predatory animal control. New Mexico District. *Annual Repts.* U.S.D.A. Bur. Biol. Surv.

_____. 1928a. Predatory animal control. New Mexico District. *Feb. Narrative.* U.S.D.A. Bur. Biol. Surv.

_____. 1928b. Predatory animal control. New Mexico District. *Mar. Narrative.* U.S.D.A. Bur. Biol. Surv.

HALL, E.R. and K.R. KELSON. 1959. *The mammals of North America.* Ronald Press, N.Y. 2:547–1083.

HOLLISTER, N.K. 1924. Some effects of environment and habitat on captive lions. *Proc. U.S. Natl. Mus.* 53:177–193.

HOUSHOLDER, B. 1968. The wolf in Arizona. 20 pp. Mimeo.

HOWARD, W.E. 1949. A means to distinguish skulls of coyotes and domestic dogs. *J. Mamm.* 30:169–171.

ILJIN, N.A. 1941. Wolf-dog genetics. *J. Genetics* 42:359–414.

KENNERLY, C.B.R. 1856. Report on the zoology of the expedition. In *Reports of exploration and surveys, etc., 1853–1854.* Vol. 4. Expedition under Lt. A.W. Whipple, Corps of Topographical Engineers, upon the route near the 35th parallel. Washington, D.C.

KNOWLTON, F.F. 1972. Preliminary interpretations of coyote population mechanics with some management implications. *J. Wildl. Manage.* 36:369–389.

KOLENOSKY, G.B. 1972. Wolf predation on wintering deer in east-central Ontario. *J. Wildl. Manage.* 36:357–368.

KOLENOSKY, G.B. and R.O. STANDFIELD. 1975. Morphological and ecological variation among gray wolves (*Canis lupus*) of Ontario, Canada. pp. 62–72, in *The wild canid: their systematics, behavioral ecology and evolution* (M.W. Fox, ed.). Van Nostrand Reinhold Co., N.Y. 508 pp.

LANDON, C.R. 1955. Predatory animal control in Texas. *Sheep and Goat Raiser,* July: 2 pp.

LANEY, L.H. 1942–1951. Predatory animal control. New Mexico District. *Annual Repts.* U.S.D.I. Fish and Wildl. Serv.

———. 1950a. Predatory animal control. New Mexico District. *Mar. Quarter Narrative.* U.S.D.I. Fish and Wildl. Serv.

———. 1951a. Predatory animal control. New Mexico District. *Dec. Quarter Narrative.* U.S.D.I. Fish and Wildl. Serv.

———. 1955–1956. Predatory animal control. New Mexico District. *Annual Repts.* U.S.D.I. Fish and Wildl. Serv.

———. 1958. Predatory animal control. New Mexico District. *Annual Rept.* U.S.D.I. Fish and Wildl. Serv.

LANGE, K.I. 1960. Mammals of the Santa Catalina Mountains, Arizona. *Amer. Midl. Nat.* 64:436–458.

LAYNE, J.N. 1954. The biology of the red squirrel, *Tamiasciurus hudsonicus loquax* (Bangs), in central New York. *Ecol. Monog.* 24:227–267.

LEOPOLD, A.S. 1949. Adios, Gavilan. *Pacific Discovery* 11:4–13.

———. 1959. *Wildlife of Mexico.* Univ. of California Press, Berkeley. 568 pp.

LIGON, J.S. 1916–1921 and 1924. Predatory animal control. New Mexico District. *Annual Repts.* U.S.D.A. Bur. Biol. Surv.

LINDSAY, E.H. and N.T. TESSMAN. 1974. Cenozoic vertebrate localities and faunas in Arizona. *J. Ariz. Acad. Sci.* 9:3–24.

LOWE, C.H. and D.E. BROWN. 1982. Introduction. In *The biotic communities of the Southwest, Desert Plants.* (D.E. Brown, ed.).

MARSH, E.G., JR. 1937. Biological survey of the Santa Rosa and Del Carmen Mountains of northern Coahuila, Mexico. U.S.D.I. Nat. Park. Serv. Report. 73 pp., photos and map.

MARTIN, P.S. 1963. *The last 10,000 years.* Univ. of Arizona Press, Tucson. 87 pp.

MARTIN, P.S. and F. PLOG. 1973. *The archaeology of Arizona—a study of the southwest region.* Amer. Mus. of Nat. Hist, Doubleday/Natural History Press, Garden City, N.Y. 391 pp.

MCBRIDE, R.T. 1977. The status and ecology of the mountain lion (*Felis concolor stanleyana*) of the Texas-Mexico border. M.S. Thesis. Dept. of Biol. Sul Ross State Univ. Alpine, Texas. 160 pp.

_____. 1978. Status of the gray wolf (*Canis lupus baileyi*) in Mexico. U.S.D.I. Fish and Wildl. Serv. Report. 72 pp.

_____. 1980. The Mexican wolf (*Canis lupus baileyi*). U.S.D.I. Fish and Wildl. Serv. Endangered Species Report 8:1–38.

MC CULLOUGH, D.R. 1971. *The tule elk, its history, behavior and ecology.* Univ. of Calif. Press, Berkeley and Los Angeles.

MECH, L.D. 1966. The wolves of Isle Royale. *U.S.D.I. Nat. Park Serv. Fauna Ser.* 7:1–210.

_____. 1970. *The wolf.* Natural History Press, Garden City, N.Y. 384 pp.

_____. 1975. Disproportionate sex ratios of wolf pups. *J. Wildl. Manage.* 39:737–740.

_____. 1977. Productivity, mortality, and population trends of wolves in northeastern Minnesota. *J. Mamm.* 58:559–574.

MERCER, E.M. 1937–1961. Predatory animal control. Arizona District. *Annual Repts.* U.S.D.A. Bur. Biol. Surv., U.S.D.I. Fish and Wildl. Serv.

MOWAT, F. 1963. *Never cry wolf.* Little, Brown, Boston. 164 pp.

MÖLLHAUSEN, H.B. 1858. *Diary of a journey from the Mississippi to the coasts of the Pacific with a United States government expedition.* 2 vols. London. 749 pp.

MURIE, A. 1944. The wolves of Mt. McKinley. *U.S.D.I. Nat. Park Serv. Fauna Ser.* 5:1–238.

MUSGRAVE, M.E. 1919–1929. Predatory animal control. Arizona District. *Annual Repts.* U.S.D.A. Bur. Biol. Surv.

NELSON, E.W. and E.A. GOLDMAN. 1929. A new wolf from Mexico. *J. Mamm.* 10:165–166.

NENTVIG, J. 1763. *Rudo Ensayo.* Trans. republished 1951. Arizona Silhouettes, Tucson.

NICHOL, A.A. 1936. Large predator animals. *Univ. Ariz. Bull.* 3:1–70.

NUNLEY, G.L. 1977. The Mexican gray wolf in New Mexico. U.S.D.I. Fish and Wildl. Serv. Report. 80 pp.

O'CONNER, J. 1939. *Game in the desert.* Derrydale Press, N.Y.

PETERSON, R.O. 1977. Wolf ecology and prey relationships on Isle Royale. *U.S.D.I. Nat. Park Serv. Sci. Monog. Ser.* 11:1–210.

PICKENS, H.D. 1980. *Tracks across New Mexico.* Bishop Publishing Co., Portales, N.M. 121 pp.

PIMLOTT, D.H. 1967. Wolf predation and ungulate populations. *Am. Zool.* 7:267–278.

———. 1969. The ecology of the timber wolf in Algonquin Provincial Park. *Ontario Dept. Lands and Forest Research Rept. (Wildl.)* 87:1–92.

PINEAU, E.L. 1923. Predatory animal control. New Mexico District. *Annual Rept.* U.S.D.A. Bur. Biol. Surv.

———. 1926. Predatory animal control. New Mexico District. *Aug. Narrative.* U.S.D.A. Bur. Biol. Surv.

POPE, E.F. 1925–1926. Predatory animal control. New Mexico District. *Annual Repts.* U.S.D.A. Bur. Biol. Surv.

_____. 1926. Predatory animal control. New Mexico District. *Aug. and Sept. Narratives.* U.S.D.A. Bur. Biol. Surv.

RASMUSSEN, D.I. 1941. Biotic communities of Kaibab Plateau, Arizona. *Ecol. Monog.* 11:229–275.

RHODES, A.P. 1940. *In* Mercer, E.M. Predatory animal control. Arizona District. 1939–1940 *Annual Repts.* U.S.D.A. Bur. Biol. Surv.

RUSSO, J.P. 1964. The Kaibab North deer herd—its history, problems and management. *Ariz. Game and Fish Dept. Wildl. Bull.* 7:1–195.

SAY, T. 1823. *In* Long's *Expedition to the Rocky Mountains* 1819–1820. U.S. Govern. Report. 2 vols. 945 pp.

SCHMIDLY, D.J. 1977. *The mammals of Trans-Pecos Texas.* Texas A & M Press, College Station. 225 pp.

SCUDDAY, J.F. 1972. Two recent records of gray wolves in west Texas. *J. Mamm.* 53:598.

_____. 1977. The Mexican gray wolf in Texas. U.S.D.I. Fish and Wildl. Serv. Report. 16 pp.

SETON, E.T. 1929. *Lives of game animals.* Doubleday, Doran and Co., Garden City, N.Y. 4 vols.

SHREVE, F. 1942. Grassland and related vegetation in northern Mexico. *Madrono* 6:190–200.

SITGREAVES, L. 1853. *Report of an expedition down the Zuni and Colorado rivers.* Robert Armstrong, Washington D.C. 190 pp.

SKEEL, M.A. and L.N. CARBYN. 1977. The morphological relationship of gray wolves (*Canis lupus*) in national parks of central Canada. *Canadian J. Zool.* 55:737–747.

SMITH, C.C. 1968. The adaptive nature of social organization in the genus of tree squirrels *Tamiasciurus. Ecol. Monog.* 38:31–63.

STEVENS, J.T. 1979. Once abundant throughout the state, wolves are now almost gone. *Texas Parks and Wildl. Dept. Leaflet* 7000–45:1–3.

TAYLOR, W.P., W.B. MCDOUGALL, C.C. PRESNALL and K.P. SCHMIDT. 1945. Preliminary ecological survey of the northern Sierra del Carmen, Coahuila, Mexico. Texas Coop. Wildl. Research Unit Report. 48 pp., photos and map.

TYLER, Daniel. 1964. *A concise history of the Mormon Battalion in the Mexican war.* The Rio Grande Press, Chicago. 376 pp.

VERME, L.J. 1969. Reproductive patterns of white-tailed deer related to nutritional plane. *J. Wildl. Manage.* 33:881–887.

VERME, L.J. and J.J. OZOGA. 1981. Sex ratio of white-tailed deer and the estrus cycle. *J. Wildl. Manage.* 45:710–715.

WAGONER, J.J. 1952. History of the cattle industry in southern Arizona, 1540–1940. *Univ. of Arizona Social Sci. Bull.* 20. Univ. of Arizona Press, Tucson.

WAUER, R.H. 1973. *Naturalist's Big Bend.* Peregrine Productions, Santa Fe. 159 pp.

WHEELER, G.H. 1875. *Report upon geographical and geological explorations and surveys west of the 100th meridian.* Washington, D.C. Vol. 5:1–1019.

WILLIAMS, C.W. 1974. *Animal tales of the West.* The Naylor Company, San Antonio. 221 pp.

WILLIAMS, O.W. 1908. Historical review of animal life in Pecos County. *Fort Stockton Pioneer* series. Distributed in booklet form by the author. 96 pp.

YOUNG, S.P. 1944. History, life habits, economic status, and control. Part I *in* Young, S.P. and E.A. Goldman, *The wolves of North America,* Amer. Wildl. Inst., Washington, D.C. pp. 1–385.

YOUNG, S.P. and E.A. GOLDMAN. 1944. *The wolves of North America.* Amer. Wildl. Inst., Washington, D.C. 636 pp.

Index